**ORTHO**

# START-TO-FINISH
# PATHS &
# WALKWAYS

Meredith® Books
Des Moines, Iowa

Ortho® Books
An imprint of Meredith® Books

**All About Paths and Walkways**
Editor: Larry Johnston
Contributing Writer: Martin Miller
Senior Associate Design Director: Tom Wegner
Assistant Editor: Harijs Priekulis
Copy Chief: Terri Fredrickson
Copy and Production Editor: Victoria Forlini
Editorial Operations Manager: Karen Schirm
Managers, Book Production: Pam Kvitne,
    Marjorie J. Schenkelberg
Contributing Copy Editor: Steve Hallam
Technical Proofreader: Dave Davis
Contributing Proofreaders: Heidi Johnson, David Krause,
    Anne Terpstra
Indexer: Barbara L. Klein
Electronic Production Coordinator: Paula Forest
Editorial and Design Assistants: Renee E. McAtee,
    Karen McFadden

**Additional Editorial Contributions from**
    **Art Rep Services**
Director: Chip Nadeau
Designer: Ik Design
Illustrator: Rick Hanson

**Meredith® Books**
Publisher and Editor in Chief: James D. Blume
Design Director: Matt Strelecki
Managing Editor: Gregory H. Kayko
Executive Editor, Gardening and Home Improvement:
    Benjamin W. Allen
Executive Editor, Home Improvement: Larry Erickson

Director, Operations: George A. Susral
Director, Production: Douglas M. Johnston
Executive Director, Sales: Ken Zagor

Vice President and General Manager: Douglas J. Guendel

**Meredith Publishing Group**
President, Publishing Group: Stephen M. Lacy
Vice President-Publishing Director: Bob Mate

**Meredith Corporation**
Chairman and Chief Executive Officer: William T. Kerr

Chairman of the Executive Committee: E.T. Meredith III

Thanks to
Rowat Cut Stone & Marble Co., Inc., Des Moines

Photographers
    (Photographers credited may retain copyright ©
    to the listed photographs.)
L = Left, R = Right, C = Center, B = Bottom, T = Top
Fran Brennan: 17BR
R. Christman: 84
Josephine Coatsworth: 68
Stephen Cridland: 3TC, 13CR, 14BL, 17TR, 22BR
Laurie Dickson: 13BR, 17CR
Richard Felber: 12TL, 71
Ed Gohlich: 11BR, 20TL, 22TL, 62, 72
Jay Graham: 6BL, 20BL
Jamie Hadley: 14TL
Jim Hedrich/Hedrich-Blessing: 12TR
Roy Inman: 10CL, 86
Jon Jensen: 9
Michael Jensen: 21CR
Pete Krumhardt: 3T, 4TL
Barbara Martin: 14CL
Julie Mavis/Semel: 11BL
Janet Mesic-Mackie: 7, 92
Mike Moreland: 8, 93
Tim Murphy/Foto Imagery: 4BR
Mary Carolyn Pindar: 6BR, 70
Portland Cement Association: 40, 68, 88, 89
Eric Roth: 80
William Stites: 10TL, 11BC
Rick Taylor: 21TR
Tom Tracy: 3B, 74
Bryan Whitney: 13TR

All of us at Ortho® Books are dedicated to providing you
with the information and ideas you need to enhance your
home and garden. We welcome your comments and
suggestions about this book. Write to us at:
    Meredith Corporation
    Ortho Books
    1716 Locust St.
    Des Moines, IA 50309–3023

If you would like to purchase any of our home improvement,
gardening, cooking, crafts, or home decorating and design
books, check wherever quality books are sold. Or visit us at:
merredithbooks.com

If you would like more information on other Ortho
products, call 800-225-2883 or visit us at: www.ortho.com

**Note to the Readers:** Due to differing conditions, tools,
and individual skills, Meredith Corporation assumes no
responsibility for any damages, injuries suffered, or losses
incurred as a result of following the information published
in this book. Before beginning any project, review the
instructions carefully, and if any doubts or questions remain,
consult local experts or authorities. Because codes and
regulations vary greatly, you always should check with
authorities to ensure that your project complies with all
applicable local codes and regulations. Always read and
observe all of the safety precautions provided by
manufacturers of any tools, equipment, or supplies,
and follow all accepted safety procedures.

## PATHWAYS TO DESIGN 4

## DESIGNING WITH MATERIALS 22

## PUTTING YOUR PATH ON PAPER 44

## CONSTRUCTION BASICS 50

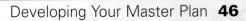

## BUILDING PATHS AND WALKWAYS 68

*Different materials lend themselves naturally to different design styles and uses. Here, brick edged with landscape timbers creates a formal look that will stand up to moving wheelbarrows and other equipment from the garden shed to the planting beds.*

## ONE STEP AT A TIME

If your budget won't let you build your dream landscape all at once, plan and install improvements as you can afford them.

A modest investment in a path, for example, can make a stunning improvement in the look of your landscape. And although it's true that hard materials—like brick and stone—can pay back their initial high cost in a long-term reduction in maintenance expenses, that doesn't put the money in your pocket now.

Consider low-cost, natural, durable, attractive materials. Pea gravel, wood rounds, and homemade stepping-stones can produce a walkway every bit as appealing as more expensive alternatives.

What's more, if you build the base of the walk to accommodate your preferred material, you can put on chips or some other less expensive top layer now, then remove it and install more expensive paving later without having to rebuild the base.

# PATHWAYS TO DESIGN

## BUILDING CODES

Almost all communities have building codes to ensure the safety, uniformity, and quality of construction methods and materials. In some communities, these codes—as well as zoning ordinances and deed restrictions—apply to landscape improvements.

They probably won't affect a single path or walkway in the backyard, but you may find your choice of materials limited when planning a new path to the front door.

A complete renovation or redesign of the landscape, including the addition of walls or fences, will probably be subject to local ordinances. To avoid problems later, check with your local zoning and building departments before you start the project to see if any restrictions apply.

**Flagstones set into the ground as stepping-stones create an informal path from the deck steps through the garden. Curves in the path and plants growing between the stones and over their edges add to this path's informal style.**

Paths and walkways tie a landscape design together; they weave among trees, structures, and planting beds, visually linking them and providing a way to travel from place to place. Because paths should be attractive and fit into the landscape, both function and aesthetics are important in their design and construction.

When you design a path, think about how you will use it and how you want it to look. You can then determine whether the path should be straight or curved, what materials to use, and how to construct it.

A standard concrete sidewalk would work just fine to go from the garage to the garden shed. But flagstone or brick could be just as functional and would be more attractive. And even concrete can be made to look beautiful with color and embossed designs.

This book will help you create paths that meet your needs and tastes. The first chapter presents hundreds of ideas for designing paths and fitting them into the landscape. The next chapter has complete descriptions of the pathway materials available. The following chapters show how to put your path design on paper, review general construction techniques, and demonstrate step-by-step methods for building your path.

# PRACTICAL PATHWAYS

Paths solve problems. They provide a way to travel from one place to another, unify the design elements of the landscape, and can reduce landscape maintenance. A path or network of paths is also a great way to add something new to a landscape without disrupting the character of the old one.

A path should have a purpose. Determining that purpose is the first thing to consider. Start by asking yourself these questions:
- How will the path be used?
- Who will use it?

The answers will help you determine the path's route through the yard and what kind of surface it should have.

## FUNCTION FIRST

Many landscapes need some strictly functional, single-purpose paths—those that simply get you from one place in the yard to another. A footpath worn into the grass is a sure sign that you probably need to put in a path or sidewalk. Walks from the house to the garage or from the garage to the garden shed are typical examples. Such paths get frequent use. They should be wide, feel comfortable and secure underfoot, and allow you to proceed quickly from one point to another.

If getting groceries from the garage to the house is the main purpose of the walk, making it meander through a cottage garden will almost ensure that people will step off the path and take short cuts through the plantings. Unless you plan to include new elements in your design, working paths like these are best laid in straight lines. (See also "Working With the Terrain" on page 8.)

If you already have a sidewalk that connects these locations but that isn't attractive, consider ways to improve its appearance.

Nonutilitarian paths can take a more circuitous route. A path joining informal flower beds, for example, might call for a design more suited to a leisurely pace. Gentle curves will slow the pace of traffic yet make it easy to move materials and equipment along the path. And if you won't need to move materials and equipment along the path, you can make it narrow and winding.

Function also affects surface and construction choices. A path for children running barefoot between the pool and the house should not be surfaced with sharp crushed quartz, rough bark, or slick tile, for instance. Stepping-stones spaced for child-size steps or brick laid in a sand bed would be a better choice.

Materials must suit the purpose of the path. If you're going to push wheelbarrows along a path, continuous hard paving will make the work easier. If the path is meant for strolling among the flowers, soft materials or stepping-stones like these are good choices.

*Paths need both a place to start and a place to end. When these features don't exist naturally in the landscape, create them. This rustic arbor marks the start of a path to a most relaxing destination— a hammock in the trees.*

If you want a path so you can wander through the gardens, but you will also be moving wheeled equipment along it, closely spaced pavers or stepping-stones are a better choice than redwood bark. A path with closely spaced stones lends itself to a leisurely stroll; placing the stones or pavers farther apart will speed up foot traffic.

## WHAT'S ALONG THE WAY?

Think of your path as part of the floor in your landscape when you pick materials.

Then think of the path as a trail when you're planning its course. A trail invites you to take a journey—it hints of the unknown, the unexpected, the mysterious. When planning a new path for your landscape, include elements that increase the interest and provide surprises along the way.

Curves—gentle or abrupt—and tall plants can hide the view around the corner, creating a sense of anticipation. The surprise can be anything you choose—a shaft of sunlight piercing through the trees and falling on a gazing ball, a water feature, or some other accent. A spectacular view always provides sufficient reward at the end of a path. Simple elements—like randomly placed

*Instead of leading to just a dead end at the fence, this path brings you to a pair of chairs— a nice place to sit in the garden.*

cut-stone stepping-stones—lead the eye along the path and entice you to follow it. Any kind of pattern will make you want to follow the path. And if you include places for resting along the way—a bench, a tree stump sawn at a height for sitting, or even a wide spot in the path—you will create a rhythm within the walk that will add to its charm.

## SOURCES OF INSPIRATION

Begin your path design by looking at how friends and neighbors have put in paths and how they have arranged the other elements in their landscape. Visit public gardens and parks too. Make sketches of things you like, and keep them in a folder.

Gardening magazines show many ideas; some are sure to fit your own sense of style and the needs of your path. You can find product literature and design ideas at home centers and landscape stores. Cut or copy photos from the magazines and take samples home from retail outlets. Put them all into the folder.

When you're ready to make decisions, spread out the results of your research on a table. Discard ideas that no longer strike your fancy or those that seem impractical. Keep the things you like and modify them to fit your own needs. Make sketches, then take them out in the yard to see how they might work in the landscape.

## MAKING THINGS EASY

Consider maintenance when planning a path.

Organic materials and loose stone need frequent upkeep and will tend to migrate into lawns and flower beds. Grass paths must be mowed. If you don't have the time or inclination to regularly maintain a path, hard materials may be a better (though a more expensive) choice. If you live in a snowy climate, will you need to use the path in the winter—to get to a garage, for instance? If so, pick a surface that you can shovel or clear with a snowblower.

If the path crosses a lawn, consider mowing. You can mow right over stepping-stones or a hard path sunk into the grass. But grass will soon grow over the edges and cover the path, so you'll need to trim and edge. Placing the surface ½ to 1 inch above grade will keep the grass at bay and make edging easier.

# PRACTICAL PATHWAYS
*continued*

*You'll enjoy your path more if it leads to a destination or place of interest. This stone path leads to an arbor and a colorful flower bed. Another path approaches from the other end.*

## WHERE DOES IT END?

Imagine walking along a path that simply ends in an open expanse of lawn or comes up to a chain link fence with the neighbor's yard just beyond. You would probably be disappointed following a path that doesn't lead to anything of interest.

Once you've started down a path, you expect it to take you somewhere. That destination can be a dramatic overlook above a river or lake, a simple herb garden, or the entrance to a vine-covered garden shed. (Even a utility shed can be charming.)

No matter what the style of your path, it should have a definite end point. Ideally, the destination should provide an experience— something to anticipate as you get closer to it.

Paths can lead to areas for family play in the yard, or they can take you through a wooded area to a secluded spot. They can lead to gazebos or other outdoor structures, or to entryways to public areas framed by pilasters or gates.

Some paths lead circuitously back to their starting point. Such paths are, in effect, ends in themselves. This is a good way to provide a destination when your landscape lacks features you consider dramatic or exciting. You may find that the lack of an astounding ocean view, for instance, doesn't matter as much when the paths in your urban backyard lead you around and through a colorful array of flower beds.

## THE HIERARCHY OF PATHS

When planning your paths, it helps to rank them in order of how frequently you use each one.

The primary path should be the one that leads to your front door. It will normally be the widest walk on the property and will often look best when installed in a formal paving style. For two people to walk comfortably side by side, a path should be at least 4 feet wide.

Secondary paths—those leading from the primary path or to side or rear entrances to the property—usually are narrower and may be paved with contrasting and more informal materials, depending on the surrounding landscape. Secondary paths generally are from 2 to 3 feet wide.

Tertiary paths are generally the least traveled, connecting other elements in the landscape. They are often (but not always) the narrowest; because they are less traveled, the materials they're made of do not have to stand up to hard use. Tertiary paths or any that are designed for one person (as stepping-stones usually are) can be from 18 to 24 inches wide.

## WORKING WITH THE TERRAIN

Natural landscapes are not perfectly flat— not even the deserts and plains we think of as flat. Variations in terrain, as well as trees, rocks, and slopes, may look like obstacles to your path, but you can turn most of them into opportunities as you plan your path.

Steep slopes, of course, can prove unsafe for any walk, but steps will make the path easier to climb and can add architectural interest. Slopes also present an opportunity to make the path more interesting. Bending your loose-stone or bark-chip path around natural features will save you time and effort in cutting into the soil and will make your path look as if Mother Nature herself put it there. Even a gentle slope can be made more appealing by running the path back and forth across it rather than straight up.

Trees and other so-called obstacles can actually help you plan informal paths. Curves look best if they have a reason to exist— if they are passing around a tree, rock, or pond, or traversing a steep slope. Random curves in a path will look confusing.

Low, boggy soil can be a poor location for a path because rainwater might not drain properly. When planning the approach to boggy areas, see if you can raise the course off the low ground and plant a bog garden along its edge. If you can place the path even slightly above the lowest spot, it will drain naturally and effectively, and you won't have to provide supplemental drainage.

*Steps make a slope easier to climb. They also break the contours of the slope and add interest to the course of the walk.*

## OPTIONS FOR REDESIGN

Decks, patios, play areas, and plantings are often significant parts of a landscape. If you're adding such improvements, your results will be more enjoyable and better looking if you approach the planning with an eye toward developing an overall landscape design.

Planning an entire landscape begins with the same exercises as planning a pathway—decide how you want to use each area or zone in the landscape, then install elements that fit those purposes. This is also an opportunity to begin looking for everyday problems you've never had the time to solve. With a little thought, you'll find these problems can turn into opportunities for design.

**DESIGN FOR EASE:** Instead of always having to move the car to get the mower out, build a storage shed. Stop trying to grow grass where it won't grow—plant shrubs or ground cover. Become familiar with the culture of plants so you can plant species that thrive naturally in your location and don't need special treatment or coaxing.

**DESIGN FOR COMFORT:** Plan your deck or patio so it isn't in direct sun at the hottest period of the day. That shaded area might not let grass grow but would work perfectly as the setting for a couple of large flagstones and a wooden bench. If you're putting a restful area in a path, make sure the location drains quickly so it doesn't become a breeding place for mosquitoes. Keep harsh winds away from your family-fun areas with tall, sturdy evergreens.

**DESIGN FOR PRIVACY:** Those evergreens can increase privacy in your yard. So can fences or walls. But be careful not to build structures that make you feel confined.

Plants and structures also give definition to areas and can visually separate them from each other. Low shrubs will keep the kids' play area or pool somewhat secluded, but leave one side open so you can keep their activities in full view. Look from inside the house too. If you never open the blinds on one wall, it's a sure sign you need exterior screening, either to shield the room from the glaring sun or to block the view.

**DESIGN FOR VIEWS:** While you're inside the house, look out and imagine how you could change the view from an open expanse of lawn to a vista that draws you out. If your yard lacks natural beauty, you can create it yourself with a well-coordinated hard scape and planting plan. See pages 44–49 for more information on planning for use.

# DESIGNING WITH PRINCIPLES

*Color plays a part in a path's design. Red brick and pink sandstone, for instance, set off foliage. Dark granite and ferns lend a dramatic air to this path.*

You probably don't think of yourself as a landscape designer and may believe you are completely unfamiliar with design elements and principles.

Yet perhaps without being aware of it, you've used design elements (color, texture, and form) and principles (unity, balance, and accent) when decorating inside your home. You can apply those same skills to the landscape design when planning paths or alterations for your yard.

## COLOR AND TEXTURE

Color and texture go together for most path materials; when you've chosen one, you've pretty much chosen the other.

Most brick, for example, is red and coarsely textured. Pine needles are usually yellow-red to reddish-orange and display a fine texture. Flagstone is coarse, and even though it comes in several varieties, the color range is limited to subdued reds, tans, and gray-blues.

Color is the element that usually grabs our attention first. Texture is tactile, and somewhat more elusive. Use color carefully. Its impact will vary greatly depending on the amount you use. A narrow red-brick path working its way through a cottage garden might provide a nice contrast with pale blossoms, while a 4-foot-wide brick walk would overpower a small yard.

In almost all cases, you can confidently use colors that already exist in your landscape. The color and style of the house and other structures—and the textures of their materials—are often the main influences in your choice of materials.

*Texture adds interest to any path. Many materials, such as stone and gravel, have inherent texture. The pattern in which the path is laid often creates texture independent of the material.*

*Paths create movement in the landscape. Straight paths give a formal look and lead to a destination quickly; curved paths are more casual and invite leisurely strolls through the garden.*

## COMPLEMENT OR CONTRAST?

Design elements either complement or contrast each other. Complementary elements have similarities or work together to form a whole. Contrasting elements have differences that are highlighted by being placed together.

These properties affect the overall appearance of your landscape. A light-colored cut-stone walk complements a bed of white roses. The same path contrasts with red tulips. Stepping-stones provide a pleasant textural contrast when set in a redwood-bark path. But on a woodland path, stones or redwood bark complement a natural setting.

## LINE

The line of a path is the course it follows through your yard. Straight lines are formal and move the view quickly from start to end, helping the viewer take in the entire design at once. Curved lines are informal and slower moving, and can create mystery. Curved lines will complement a sinuous planting bed and separate it from paving. Straight lines might look best setting off an angular walk from the lawn. Line also leads the eye and contributes to the style of your design.

## PATHS WITH PRINCIPLE

Rather than treat your path as a single element, integrate it with the landscape. A formal brick path looks more at home leading to a stately two-story red-brick house than a path surfaced with pine needles or bark. But organic materials would look just fine with a stone or faded-brick structure. A wood boardwalk or a rough-textured material would be an ideal look for a path leading across a meadowed lawn to a free-standing rustic summerhouse. Likewise, if

### THE SAFEST PATH

To make sure that traversing your path won't be a risky venture, design with safety in mind.
- Textured surfaces reduce the potential of slips and falls. Use coarse-textured materials, especially in locations likely to get wet. Broom-finish concrete to make it safe.
- Build steps up steep slopes instead of sloping the path.
- Use flat stones and slope the walk slightly to one side so water drains off instead of forming puddles. Puddles are hazards in warm weather, treacherous when they freeze.
- Remove clutter frequently.
- Install low-voltage lights on paths and steps used at night.
- Include elements such as different-size paving stones or materials of different colors that signal an upcoming change of level.

you're putting in a rock garden, you may want loose stones or flagstone leading up to—and perhaps surrounding—it.

By carefully manipulating the color, texture, and line of your pathway, you will make it an integral landscape element.

## OPTIONS FOR REDESIGN

Planning a renovated landscape will present you with more challenges than laying out a single path. Making large-scale improvements means using color, texture, line, and form to make a cohesive design.
- Unity is the principle that ties everything together. Repeating a color or texture—using the same brick in a patio and path, for

example—is an effective way to achieve unity.
- Balance among elements can be symmetrical, with straight paths and geometric patterns, or asymmetrical, with curved lines, irregular shapes, and odd-numbered groupings.
- Accent adds surprises or calls attention to an element. It's the spice of design. An accent can be a small

antique yard ornament or a large fountain. It's where you place an accent that counts—it must go where it draws attention to itself. This often works best against a neutral background.

These photographs show paths combined with other elements. Each arrangement is different, yet each design is useful and attractive.

# DESIGNING WITH STYLE

*Almost any materials and edgings can be used to create a path that fits a formal setting perfectly. The straight lines of this grass path and the two arbors are carefully arranged in this formal style.*

*A curved path and less-manicured plantings alongside make this landscape informal. The sundial, statue, and lamppost serve as surprises along the path.*

One of the quickest ways to become familiar with questions of style—and to begin moving in a direction that reflects your personality—is to divide style into two categories: formal and informal. Think about the way you live and your tastes, and you'll probably know immediately which camp you're in.

■ Formal design schemes have straight lines, right angles, geometric shapes, and even-numbered groupings. Formality creates a sense of regularity and symmetry. Paths laid at right angles to each other will impart a formal air.

■ Informal styles have curved lines, irregular shapes, and odd-numbered, asymmetrical groupings. Informal designs often seem to create a sense of the unexpected. A cottage-style home or a bungalow may be the perfect spot for curving a path around existing flower beds. Or you can lay the beds out with sinuous edges, if they're not there already.

## MATERIALS AND STYLE

Although the contour of a path defines its style more than its materials, certain materials relate innately to certain styles because of their shape and composition.

Brick and cut-stone walks tend to be formal, especially with cut-stone edging set in repeated symmetrical patterns. Edging any material with landscape timbers looks formal.

Organic materials and loose rock are informal by nature. You can enhance their effect by building the path without edging and letting the material spill out into the surrounding beds.

The irregular edges of flagstone add a perfect informal element when set as stepping-stones. Containing the flagstone with straight-lined borders and mortaring between the stones will make it more formal.

Concrete has no innate style, but it can be curved, stamped, and colored in any pattern to meet any stylistic requirements. Wood

## PATHS IN SMALL GARDENS/YARDS

Paths can make a small area seem bigger. One way is to force perspective by narrowing the line of sight through a small space, as shown in the illustration. The stepping-stones that curve around the house make this space seem larger by suggesting a connection with an unseen area. Small plants in the background and large ones in the foreground enhance the effect, as do coarse textures in front, fine ones toward the rear.

In this way, a simple courtyard with vine-covered trellises becomes a cozy garden getaway in an urban backyard.

## GETTING DESIGN HELP

Design professionals can often see solutions to problems at a glance. Enlisting their help, in fact, can save you money in the long run. If a conference with a landscape pro results in a solution that avoids grading a slope, for example, the consultation has paid for itself. Here's a brief summary of the levels of design help you'll find in the profession.

■ Landscape architects have the most formal training and are licensed. They can handle all aspects of planning and construction supervision.

■ Landscape designers tend to have strong horticultural backgrounds, but are skilled in other aspects of design as well. They can help you draw up plans. Some can give construction advice and supervise work.

■ Nursery and garden center staff can give you suggestions on general ideas, particularly about plants and materials.

paths, however, even when constructed along formal lines, retain their informality. Wood almost always fits well with wooden structures and in rustic settings.

## MIXING THINGS UP

Even though concepts of formality and informality seem mutually exclusive, you can still have both in your landscape. The trick to merging styles is to transition one gradually into the other. Your immediate backyard may look best with formal paths and beds, but an arbor at the far end of a formal garden can mark a change of style to an organic path that leads to a wooded area.

## OPTIONS FOR REDESIGN

Although formal and informal are useful terms for describing the general attributes of a landscape, you don't have to adhere strictly to one or the other. Most landscapes will fall broadly into one style or the other while still allowing a wide margin for variations. What matters when adding new elements to the design—a path or a patio, for example—is that you keep the design of the elements generally consistent with one another.

If your paths intersect at corners, for example, that means the planting beds will probably be square or rectangular—formal shapes. Curved paths go best with informal, irregular beds. Meticulously pruned shrubs—especially if they are arranged on opposite sides of the landscape as mirror images—are a classic formal scheme. A wood deck with modern lines next to a cut-stone patio looks sleek and modern, and you can enhance that effect with geometric accents.

Styles that relate to eras (colonial or contemporary) or regions (Southwest or Mediterranean) may be either formal or informal. A style that reflects where you live is usually a safe choice. Native materials will save you money, and native plants may be easier to maintain. You also can match the landscape style to your house style.

To organize the design elements into a cohesive whole, look at your yard and divide it into imaginary zones. Divide the space along natural lines or features, such as the lay of the land, tree lines, existing planting beds, or structures. Then plan uses for each area. You may want one for entertaining, another for children's play, and another for gardening. Decide which features you could add to fulfill those uses, and design them to fit your style concept.

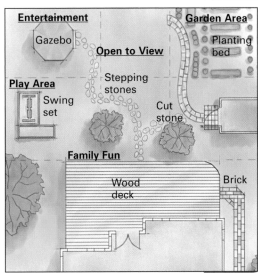

# PLANTING YOUR PATH

*A labyrinthine brick path with a variety of low-growing plants highlights this front yard. The space was once an ordinary lawn with a straight sidewalk across the middle.*

Plants and paths are natural partners. At a minimum, foliage brings a pleasing contrast in both color and texture to the path materials. But the delight of a flower-lined path doesn't stop there. Plants link the path to the surrounding landscape, they civilize what could otherwise be a featureless path, and they soften hard edges.

The colors of blossoms and foliage and the texture of the plants offer plentiful opportunities to add complements or contrasts to your design. Even if you're building a path you consider strictly functional, you might as well make it beautiful too.

## SELECTING PLANTS

Selecting plants for your path is mostly a matter of personal preference.

You might limit your plantings to contrasts—white blooms edging brick, gray leaves along a dark red flagstone, blue flowers next to the muted tan of sandstone. Or you could go entirely with complements— red variegated leaves along the brick walk, silvery foliage dotting a gravel path, or blues along slate or gray-blue stamped concrete.

What is most important in choosing plants is to understand the planting culture—the conditions of the soil, light, and water—and find plants that will thrive in the conditions in your landscape.

Plants native to your area will have a greater chance of success than exotic plants. But they are not the only choices. Your garden center can help you choose the right ones.

*Plants along the edges make even the most utilitarian walk look better. For an informal look, let the plantings grow over the edge. Move the plants around while they're still in containers to find the best arrangement.*

The lists on the opposite page show just a few plants suitable for planting along paths in sunny or shady areas. The Zone designation represents the areas of the country in which the plant will do best, based on climatic conditions in the region. The map on page 94 shows the Zones.

*These stone steps become a natural-looking part of the landscape by adding ground covers, including wooly and pineapple thyme and mother of thyme.*

## PLANTING IN THE GAPS

Placing plants in the gaps between stepping stones is a natural. A number of low-growing species will stand up to foot traffic, and some will release their fragrance when stepped on.

## PLANTS FOR SUNNY PATHS

| Common/Botanical Name | Height | Color | Zone | Comments |
|---|---|---|---|---|
| Alpine lady's mantle / *Alchemilla alpina* | 6" | Chartreuse | 3–4 | Quick to spread |
| Rockcress / *Arabis caucasica* | 8" | White | 4–8 | Mat forming |
| Sea thrift / *Armeria maritima* | 6" | Pink/White | 3–8 | Tall flower stalks |
| Carpathian bellflower / *Campanula carpatica* | 9–12" | Violet/White | 3–8 | Fast growing, clump forming |
| Plumbago / *Ceratostigma plumbaginoides* | 8" | Blue | 5–8 | Good ground cover |
| Cheddar pink / *Dianthus gratianopolitanus* | 6" | Pink | 3–9 | Mat forming, heat tolerant, fragrant |
| Aspen daisy / *Erigeron speciosus* var. *macranthus* | 8" | Lavender | 2–8 | Good for crevices, steps |
| Dwarf blue fescue / *Festuca glauca* | 8" | Silvery foliage | 4–8 | Grows in tufts for textural contrast |
| Cranesbill / *Geranium sanguineum striatum* | 8" | Light pink | 4–6 | A virtually carefree ground cover |
| Creeping baby's breath / *Gypsophila repens* | 6–9" | White/Lilac | 3–7 | Makes dramatic contrast at edges |
| Evergreen candytuft / *Iberis sempervirens* | 6–10" | White | 3–8 | Heat tolerant |
| Sword-leaf inula / *Inula ensifolia*, 'Compacta' | 10" | Yellow | 4–8 | Long-lasting flowers |
| Moss phlox / *Phlox subulata* | 6" | Pink/Lavender/White | 3–9 | Moss-like foliage, evergreen mats |
| Himalayan fleece flower / *Polygonum affine* | 6–9" | Creamy white | 4–9 | Tolerates some foot traffic |
| Soapwort / *Saponaria officinalis* | 2–3" | Rose-pink | 4–7 | Mat forming, virtually pest free |
| Sedum / *Sedum spectabile*, 'Vera Jameson' | 10–12" | Dusky pink | 3–10 | Long-season interest |
| Wild thyme / *Thymus serpyllum* | 1–8" | White/Pink/Violet | 3–8 | Four-season interest, virtually pest free |
| Creeping verbena / *Verbena* hybrids | 12" | Purple | 6–10 | All-season blooms |

Although the ideal soil conditions vary from plant to plant, the general planting procedures will be the same. You will probably find it easier to plant in the gaps as you lay the path because lifting and removing stones can be difficult. Set the stone, remove the bedding materials at its edge, and replace them with a soil mix appropriate to the plant. Check with your garden center staff about the specific soil mix for your plantings.

## PLANTS FOR SHADED PATHS

| Common/Botanical Name | Height | Color | Zone | Comments |
|---|---|---|---|---|
| Lady's mantle / *Alchemilla mollis* | 12" | Chartreuse | 4–8 | Moderate growth rate |
| Dwarf goatsbeard / *Aruncus aethusifolius* | 2" | White | 4–8 | Flowers spike above foliage mounds |
| *Astilbe* hybrid, 'Inshirach Pink' | 10" | Pink | 4–8 | Deep green foliage |
| Yellow corydalis / *Corydalis lutea* | 6–12" | Butter-yellow | 5–10 | Spreads rapidly |
| Barrenwort / *Epimedium* × *rubrum* | 10" | Red | 5–8 | Slow spreader, long interest |
| Hosta / *Hosta nakaiana*, 'Golden Tiara' | 8–12" | Purple | 3–9 | Small, gold, heart-shaped leaves |
| Dwarf crested iris / *Iris cristata* | 6" | Pale blue | 3–8 | Excellent for dry shade |
| Forget-me-not / *Myosotis scorpioides* | 6–8" | Light blue | 3–8 | Rapid growth rate |
| Woodland phlox / *Phlox divaricata* | 8" | Blue | 4–8 | Best for color |
| English primrose / *Primula vulgaris* | 6" | Yellow | 4–8 | Easy to grow, deep-veined leaves |
| Bethlehem sage / *Pulmonaria saccharata* | 12" | Blue | 3–7 | Speckled foliage |
| Meadow rue / *Thalictrum kiusianum* | 4–6" | Lavender | 4–9 | Gray-green foliage |
| Allegheny foam flower / *Tiarella cordifolia* | 6" | White/Pale pink | 3–8 | Tolerates light foot traffic |
| Sweet violet / *Viola odorata* | 8" | Violet/Rose/White | 6–8 | Best for fragrance |

# EVALUATING YOUR SITE

Before you decide the location of your path, evaluate your site. After a rain, do the neighbor kids come by to splash in a big puddle in your yard? Are trees casting shade in the right areas? Does the proposed route of your path take it up steep inclines? All of these factors—soil, sun, shade, and slope—can affect path location.

## TESTING THE SOIL

Loose, loamy soil drains well but can erode easily. Clay sheds water, can increase runoff, and may require additional drainage solutions.

How fast your soil drains will affect the base of your path. You want the water to drain off quickly and not pond on the surface.

To test drainage, dig a hole 1 foot deep and about as wide. Fill the hole with water and let it drain. Then fill it again and record how long it takes for the water to drain completely.

If the water empties in less than 12 hours, your soil drains well and you need only about 4 inches of gravel for the path base. If the water takes longer than that, you need more gravel. Add 1 to 2 inches of gravel for every 12 hours it takes the water to drain. Install a drainpipe in gravel bases 6 inches deep or deeper. In most cases, these rough estimates will prove adequate, but they may need adjustment for harsh winter conditions. For example, in the northern states, where winters are long and cold, you may need an 8-inch gravel base to keep the path from

## ONE CALL DOES IT ALL

Before starting any excavation, find the utility lines. A cut electric, phone, or gas line creates a major disruption and can pose serious dangers. Before you dig, call each utility company and have them flag the location of the lines. Most utilities will do this at no cost, and many larger cities have a unified service so you can have all the lines checked with one call. Call your utility companies to arrange for the service.

**EVALUATING YOUR SITE**

Sunlight

Path avoids lowest part of yard to prevent freezing in low areas and to avoid steep climb.

Trees shade relaxation area.

Stepping-stones at top of rise reduce angle of ascent.

Wind currents down slope create frost conditions in winter. Rainwater collects in low areas of lawn.

Level ground for play equipment

Shrubs diffuse strong wind currents.

cracking in the cold. Local building department officials can give you specific information.

## SUN AND SHADE

The way the sun falls on your property and the shade patterns cast by buildings and trees can affect the placement of your path. Notice how the sun moves across your yard at various times of the day, especially during the season you're most likely to use the path. If the purpose of your path is to go from one area to the other, shade may not be of much concern. But if you're planning flower beds and a path from which to enjoy them, sunlight can be critical, not only for the flowers but for your comfort as well.

## SLOPE

Slope affects the way a path drains, and you can take advantage of the natural drainage patterns in your yard. To determine the flow of water downhill, throw fine sand, mulch, or lime down the middle of the path site. Go out after a rain and see how the material has run off. Lay the path out to shed water toward a drainage system. On cross-slope runs, slope the surface of the path to the downhill side at 1 percent. (See pages 58–61.)

## MICROCLIMATES

Microclimates are small areas in the yard that have their own peculiar conditions. Low areas, for example, can freeze more quickly because cool air is heavier and flows downhill faster. Winds coming over a fence can make an area cooler than the ambient temperature. Localized shade can keep things damp and promote algae growth.

Don't avoid these areas; make allowances for them. Dark-colored materials in a low area will absorb sunlight and may keep surface moisture from freezing. Tall shrubs will break up wind currents and still define the edges of a private retreat. In the shade, moss or algae will be less slippery on rough textures. Treat wood regularly with preservatives.

## OPTIONS FOR REDESIGN

Site analysis for a complete landscape redesign must be more detailed than one for building a simple path.

Look at one section of the yard at a time: the front, the back, and each side. For each section, make a list of the problems you find. Is the front walk wide enough for two people to pass or walk side by side? Does the walk invite visitors toward the front door? Is this the walk that the family uses to enter the house? Or do you step off of it and travel across unpaved areas of the lawn?

Take pictures of each yard from several different angles. Look out the second-story windows in the back. Are the views appealing? Is there a view that might be better if you remove a tree or two?

Inventory access points. Do interior and exterior spaces relate to each other? Can you conveniently enter the area planned for entertaining from the living room, family room, or kitchen? Do the paths in the yard really connect elements in the landscape, or do they meander off with no clear destination?

Do you have enough privacy? Where do views from the street or the neighbors' yards intrude upon your privacy?

Note everything that needs improvement, but don't decide immediately on specific solutions. Those will come later.

Pay close attention to assets too. Identify the views you want to keep, the plantings and trees you find attractive, or contours in the terrain where you could install a deck or patio.

When you've completed a thorough inventory, make your notes on a site analysis—a scaled plan of your yard drawn on paper (see page 47). You will rely on this plan to keep all the changes cohesive.

# PATHS FOR PROBLEM AREAS

Establishing coherence is the key to good landscape design, and paths are a useful tool for creating coherence. Whether you're trying to renovate an existing design or are starting from scratch, your paths will be a critical ingredient in helping all the elements relate to one another.

Start by looking at the lines in the landscape. The first step in creating coherence is to establish lines of correspondence.

## LINES OF CORRESPONDENCE

All the lines of paths, planting beds, and other elements must relate to one another with a logical scheme. This logic need not be dramatic or even apparent.

Take a look at your planting beds. Does the shape of one relate to the others, especially those nearest it? For example, do the lines of straight beds and paths run parallel to each other, or do they fall slightly short of parallel? If there's a reason for straight lines to converge, that's OK. But if such convergence doesn't look planned, or if it does not occur in regular increments, the lines will merely look sloppy.

What about curved beds? Do the edges of one bed curve in a way that mirrors the edges of another? Such correspondences in informal design do not have to be mirror images of one another. Even the suggestion of a concave curve opposite a convex curve will often be enough. Such subtle variations improve the appeal of the design because they introduce variety into the overall unity of the design.

## VARIETY IN A UNIFIED DESIGN

Variety is an important ingredient, even in formal landscapes. You can introduce variety by changing the size—but not the rectangular shape—of the beds, or by pairing beds of different sizes on opposite sides of the yard. You can even mix different sizes together, keeping an equal number of beds on either side of an axis. Vary the width of the paths between the beds, keeping them at right angles to maintain formality.

Informal planting beds are often kidney shape, but varying the sizes and shapes of the beds will improve the overall effect of the design. And don't forget the borders of your yard. Even though the outer edge of a shrub border will probably be straight along the lot line, the interior edge should be curved to correspond to informal paths.

## POSITIVE AND NEGATIVE SPACE

Scale—the relationship of sizes within a landscape—is important; the ideas of *positive space* and *negative space* can be useful in achieving proper scale. Positive space contains an element of one kind or another,

**USING PATHS TO UNIFY A FORMAL DESIGN**

Formal planting beds

Hedge

Brick paths

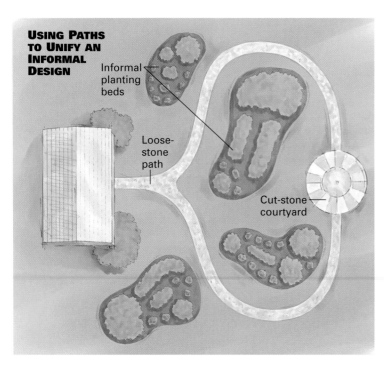

**USING PATHS TO UNIFY AN INFORMAL DESIGN**

Informal planting beds

Loose-stone path

Cut-stone courtyard

## SCALING POSITIVE AND NEGATIVE SPACE

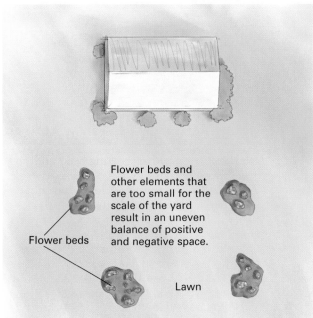

Flower beds and other elements that are too small for the scale of the yard result in an uneven balance of positive and negative space.

Flower beds

Lawn

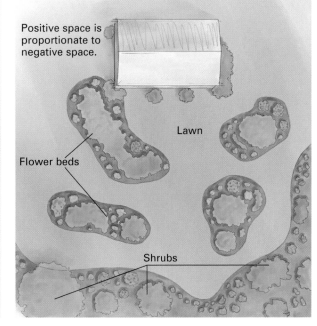

Positive space is proportionate to negative space.

Flower beds

Lawn

Shrubs

such as a planting bed, deck, or gazebo. Negative space is essentially empty. Positive space draws our eye to it because there's something going on in it. The role of negative space is to provide a foil or background for the positive spaces and to unify them.

What's important in considering these concepts is that the two kinds of spaces be appropriately scaled. They don't have to occupy the same amount of area, but they should be proportionate to each other.

Visualizing scale is easily done by looking from an upper-story window, with a family member moving garden hoses or stakes around in the yard. To make decisions of scale more precise and easier, draw a dimensioned plan (see page 44).

Plans on paper will give you a miniature bird's-eye view of the yard and allow you to experiment with lines, shapes, and proportions. Although there are no strict rules that govern landscape proportions, you can start with a 3-to-4 relationship between positive and negative space, then make adjustments to get the best appearance.

## A REASON FOR EVERYTHING

Your overall plan—even if formal—should have a certain natural quality to it, but this does not happen by accident. It is the result of looking carefully at the elements and finding ways of keeping them visually connected.

Start with the hard scape elements, such as walks, structures, and decks. Look at how they relate to other elements in your yard—both those that exist now and the ones you're planning. A square, rectangular, or angled deck or patio might inspire the development of an overall formal design. A curved flagstone entertainment area could suggest the planting of informal beds. The predominant style will help you determine whether you want an Arts and Crafts gazebo in the back or one embellished with Victorian bric-a-brac.

This doesn't mean you're locked into the existing elements—only that you should consider their shape and proportions before making final decisions. Otherwise you might never think of enlarging old, amoeba-shaped flower beds to accommodate a formal design or making them bigger for better scale in a large informal landscape. If the relationships don't already exist, you can create them with little expense and effort. Many times all it takes is a shovel.

Lines should curve for a reason. Path lines flowing around trees, the lower contours of slopes, or the edges of flower beds make sense. Paths that curve without any reason can appear distracting. If you already have such a curve, plant a tree or shrub grouping.

When a path skirts a tree, you can route the path outside the tree's drip line (the outer edge of the foliage, where rain drips off the tree) to reduce tree debris on the path. Place it far enough away that water running off the tree won't flood the path. Or you can run the path under the tree for shade and shelter.

# PATHS FOR PROBLEM AREAS
*continued*

*Angles add interest to a path through a narrow side yard, as shown above and at right. Pergolas and plantings in conjunction with the path bring beauty to an often overlooked part of a home landscape. Fencing turns the space into a private retreat.*

## THE DEVELOPMENT HOME

The tract home, the development house, or any newly built structure usually has only the barest landscaping, if any at all. These homes often suffer from narrow side yards, small areas for family fun, lack of privacy, and an overall absence of individuality.

Address the major problems first. Tall evergreen shrubs or woven fences can take care of privacy problems with little effort and cost. Such additions may also provide the defining lines for a patio or deck. Joining the side and backyards together with a path can make the side yards seem bigger. Put this small space to use by planting an herb garden.

Make the front entryway showy or subdued, but give it some kind of personality. If the garage is attached, you may not use the front door often, but you'll want friends and neighbors to feel invited.

Change the door design and add shrubs and flowering plants along the front walk. If the walk doesn't fit the style of the house, tear it up and use the pieces for low-bed borders or a retaining wall. Install a secondary walk off the front walk, leading to the side yard, to create an arbored entrance.

## THE SIDE YARD

Side yards often are treated as an afterthought. They are generally used less than front or backyards, are often smaller, and seem to demand less attention. No side yard, however, is too small to warrant abandoning the principles of design. The easiest solution for landscaping this problem area is to give it one or more useful purposes.

Narrow side yards are perfect for storage or for pets. If conveniently close to a garden area, a side yard is a great place to build a garden shed in a style that harmonizes with the house. Such a location will often be within easy reach of the garage or basement entry too.

If the shed solution won't work, plant a garden or create a cozy spot for a bedroom patio and secluded breakfasts. A small patio off a kitchen can make summer family meals more intimate.

If these options aren't appealing, consider building a fence and gate at the front of the side yard. The fence and gate will enhance the illusion that the area has a purpose, even if it's no more than a passageway from front to back. You can enhance that basic purpose by putting in a path. If nothing else, it will look more intentional than worn down grass. Colorful flower beds on either side of the walk will make the area more attractive. Be sure to watch for shade. If the yard is in shadows most of the day, you have an ideal spot for a beautiful shade garden. Choose your plants accordingly (see page 15).

Visual illusions can make the side lot seem larger. Set low, narrow beds at the edge of the property line, and make the bed lines converge slightly from the entry to the back. Put in screening plantings only if privacy requires them. If you must increase privacy, screening with plants will make you feel less closed in than a fence will.

## THE LARGE YARD

Large yards can pose more of a challenge than small ones. Small yards don't lack opportunities for intimacy; large yards may. Also, you're faced with the question of expense, which is often best answered by planning the landscape in stages, installing improvements as you go. That's why a large yard requires planning to achieve long-term coherence. You may be tempted to install a deck right away to take care of your immediate entertainment needs, but you will find your results more pleasing if you plan the entire landscape before you put in the deck.

To make planning a large project easier, divide it into jobs to do now and jobs to do later. Divide the first tasks into immediate and near-future projects.

To visually contain the part of the yard you will do first, you can plant border trees or shrubs, leaving frequent spaces along the line to suggest entrances into the area beyond. Further divisions in the yard may incorporate this same strategy to make them look separate from one another.

Make sure the transitions from one area to another are gradual and make sense. Coherence may seem harder to achieve in a large yard, but good scaling will help. Remember that each individual planting bed does not have to be huge. It's the total area occupied by beds that is more important in achieving a balanced scale.

## THE HOUSE ON THE CORNER

Corner lots often leave the house set back in an expanse of lawn. They also invite a diagonal shortcut from one sidewalk to the other, and lack privacy. Here's a chance to incorporate the techniques used for designing both side yards and large areas.

Take care of privacy and noise first. Set screening shrubs along the corners; they'll help solve both problems. Ornament the corner with a tree or flower bed—either with or without the screening plants— to slow down the short cutters and break up the expanse of empty lawn. You also can set

In a large yard, you can carry your path over a bridge spanning either a natural or constructed feature, such as this dry stream.

Gardens and a path around the perimeter emphasize the sweep of this large yard and capitalize on the splendid view.

tiered plantings on timber or other low retaining walls. Or go all the way and enclose the yard in high shrubs. If you have the room, you can create a fantastic enclosed garden setting with a front yard path surrounded by sinuous or formal beds and secondary paths leading to the rear. Add a front gate to the mix to enhance the sense of mystery.

Of course you can enclose almost any yard, but the normally wide expanse of a corner lot makes this solution seem more intriguing.

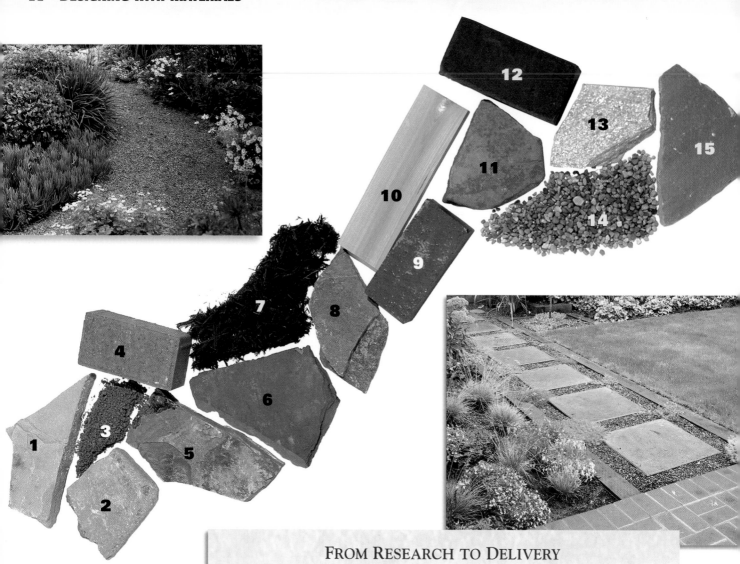

*Balance aesthetics with practical considerations such as cost and durability when selecting path material. Make your path of just one material, as shown at top, or combine materials, as shown above right. Some path materials are (1) Arizona flagstone, (2) tumbled Connecticut bluestone, (3) decomposed granite, (4) concrete brick, (5) three-rivers flagstone, (6) black slate, (7) eucalyptus mulch, (8) Connecticut bluestone, (9) clay brick, (10) cedar board, (11) tumbled Connecticut bluestone in lilac color, (12) klinker brick, (13) gold quartzite, (14) pea gravel, and (15) Iron Mountain flagstone.*

## FROM RESEARCH TO DELIVERY

Choosing the right materials for your project will be easier if you organize your search. Work from the general to the specific—start with the information in this book and augment it with some hands-on research.

Once you have a general idea of the kind of materials you'd like to use for your path, visit landscape and garden centers and home centers to see the materials firsthand. Contact paving contractors, brick and stone dealers, and concrete companies; they may have showrooms or samples you can see. You'll generally find knowledgeable staff to answer questions about material use and quantities you'll need. Many manufacturers and retailers maintain Internet sites with facts about material, use, and cost.

Ask about materials native to your area. Some materials shown in this book may be expensive or hard to get in some areas. Materials available locally will save

considerably on delivery costs. When you've narrowed things down to a few choices, bring samples home to help you visualize how textures and colors will work in your path. Find out about delivery arrangements and order about 5 percent more material (10–15 percent more for flagstone) than the actual surface calculations indicate you need.

Schedule delivery so your materials arrive after you've prepared the site. That way they won't be in the way, and you can get them delivered right to the work area, avoiding the backbreaking task of moving them yourself from a temporary storage area.

Check out dealers' return policies too. Most suppliers will accept returns of unopened bagged materials and modular items, such as brick (in sizable quantities). Poured concrete, of course, can't be returned—make sure you precisely compute your estimates for unreturnable materials.

# DESIGNING
# WITH MATERIALS

*Perhaps no other aspect of your project— with the possible exception of standing back and admiring your completed handiwork— will prove as rewarding as deciding on the materials to use. The right choice of materials, more than any other design element, will bring your pathway into harmony with the overall architecture of your yard, unifying it and complementing all of its features.*

*Because of homeowners' increased interest in landscape design, most retail outlets now have knowledgeable individuals on staff who can help you choose materials appropriate to your design. The information in this chapter will also help make the decisions easier.*

*Materials for garden-path surfaces fall into two categories—loose (or soft) materials, and hard materials. Loose or soft materials include pine needles, bark chips, grass, gravel, and crushed stone. Hard materials include natural flagstone, cut stone, brick and concrete.*

*Each material has different textures, colors, and aesthetic qualities that will affect your decision. But don't base your choice on beauty alone. Consider practicality too. Take into account your skill level, budget, and the time you want to devote to the project, both in its initial installation and in ongoing maintenance.*

*Loose materials usually require less skill and less time to install than hard materials. Soft paths also cost less, but they can require significant maintenance. Most hard-surface paths are more difficult to install and more*

*costly, but their initial investment can be returned many times over in reduced maintenance.*

*You will find all the information you need to make informed choices in this chapter. Each section summarizes the design aspects of the material, its advantages and disadvantages, climatic concerns, siting considerations, and maintenance requirements. Also, you'll find information about construction methods and estimating quantities, along with tips on where to buy the material and how it is sold or packaged.*

## PUBLIC AND PRIVATE SPACES

Your landscape contains two kinds of space—public and private. Consider the difference when choosing materials or altering your landscape design.

Public space is any area open to public view—in most cases the front yard or sections of it. Private spaces are those closed off to the public. Major changes to public spaces can affect the entire neighborhood, so if you are making improvements to your front yard, study your neighborhood's predominant style, especially that of adjacent properties.

Some neighborhoods don't have obvious boundaries between properties. Materials and plantings that maintain the open, sweeping effect will look harmonious. Other areas convey a strong regional flair. Native materials and plants will enhance that effect.

Two approaches help make choices easier:
■ If the neighborhood style is consistent, what can you do to maintain it?
■ If the style is a patchwork of varied effects, what can you do to keep the potential hodgepodge to a minimum?

# ORGANIC MATERIALS

**Wood chips**

Organic materials make attractive, low-cost paths and require only the ability to use a shovel and a rake.

Organic paths are among the least costly of all surfaces, and they adapt themselves to a variety of landscape styles. Although they are commonly considered casual, rustic, or informal (and they are certainly well suited to such installations), they can create a definite formal look when laid out in straight lines with regular borders.

The term *organic materials* encompasses a variety of products: Pine needles, wood mulch, wood chips, straw, and crushed seed hulls are the most common. Wood species available as mulches or chips include pine, oak, redwood, cedar, cypress, white birch, and, in some areas, hemlock.

## DESIGN EFFECT/SITING

■ Color and texture—Colors range from light (straw and most wood chips) to red (some barks, redwood chips, and pine needles), to dark brown (most barks and crushed seed hulls).
■ Siting—Most commonly used to create informal pathways in conjunction with gentle curves and in woodland or rustic garden settings. Will enhance a formal design in straight paths with brick or timber borders.
■ Excellent as a base material under children's outdoor play equipment (but requires frequent leveling).

## ADVANTAGES

■ Among the easiest of paths to construct.
■ Conform readily to minor variations in terrain.
■ Provide a soft, springy surface for comfortable walking and for kneeling when working in your planting beds.

**Straw**

**Crushed shells**

## DISADVANTAGES

■ Organic materials tend to be displaced with use and in heavy rains (needles and bark especially). Usually require a border to keep them contained—a must on slopes.
■ Ground or crushed materials, especially mulches, easily track into the home.
■ Subject to weed invasion (especially by airborne seeds), even over landscape fabric.
■ Paths of organic materials are often difficult to roll wheeled equipment over.
■ Organic materials break down over time and require replenishment.
■ Some seed hulls give off an unpleasant odor when wet.

## DURABILITY AND MAINTENANCE

■ Durability varies with use and material. Heavier material, such as bark and redwood chips, knit together in a carpet and will stand

**Pine needles**

**Bark mulch**

up to harder use than mulches and needles.
■ Redwood, cypress, and cedar are naturally resistant to insects and rot and will outlast other materials.
■ Most organic materials decompose and require additional materials— all require periodic raking to level them.
■ Generally suitable for most climates, although they may not dry out between rains in regions with heavy rainfall.
■ Elasticity allows them to weather freeze/thaw cycles well.

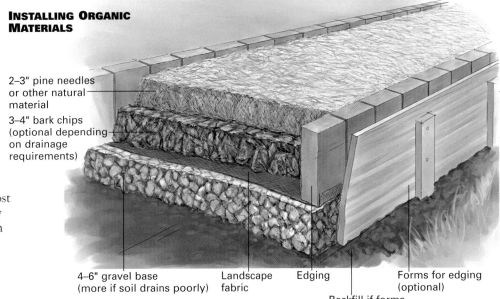

**INSTALLING ORGANIC MATERIALS**

2–3" pine needles or other natural material

3–4" bark chips (optional depending on drainage requirements)

4–6" gravel base (more if soil drains poorly)

Landscape fabric

Edging

Forms for edging (optional)

Backfill if forms are kept in place

## HOW TO INSTALL

■ Remove existing sod, then excavate soil to a depth consistent with soil drainage requirements. Install edging and landscape fabric. Pour and level base material, then topping. (See illustration, right. Installation instructions are on page 70.) For a quick, simple path, dig 2–3 inches deep, crowning the base in the middle slightly. Then lay landscape fabric over the soil, and pour in the topping material.

## HOW ORGANIC MATERIALS ARE SOLD

■ Buy these materials by the bale, bag (cubic foot), or truckload.
■ In some regions, some materials such as pine needles may be hard to find, but you can order them from landscape catalogs or Internet retailers.
■ For small projects, order bagged materials. To save money on large installations, order by the truckload, if possible. A standard pickup truck will carry about 2 cubic yards of material.

## ESTIMATING QUANTITIES

■ Determine the volume of the excavated pathway. Order by cubic yard (divide volume in cubic feet by 27) or cubic foot. A cubic yard of material will fill a 27-foot path that is 4 feet wide and 3 inches deep.
■ Baled material coverage varies with material. One bale of pine needles will fill 10 cubic feet (40 square feet, 3 inches deep), but other products will not go as far. Check with your supplier for accurate estimates.
■ A cubic yard of wood bark will normally cover an area of about 100 square feet.

## WHERE TO BUY ORGANIC MATERIALS

■ Buy these materials at garden centers and landscape dealers. Also check with local landscape firms, government forestry offices, utility companies, and local sawmills for wood chips. Local supplies will cost much less than bagged material at a garden center but may have uneven texture and unattractive strips.
■ Local farms or co-ops may collect materials for resale. (Wood chips bought by the truckload may include twigs and branches.)

## DESIGN TIPS

Organic materials lend themselves to informal designs and look best with uncomplicated contours. Lay out the path where you would walk around the natural elements of your terrain—trees, rocks, and streams.

Although laying out the path on paper will help you define its contours, always check your design against the real landscape before you begin installing it, especially if you're putting the pathway in a woodland area. Relying on paper plans alone may cause you to miss exciting natural details—moss-covered rocks, outcroppings, or flowers growing in the shade.

Combine organic materials with others to add interest, especially in an urban setting. Install wood rounds or homemade concrete stepping-stones and surround them with needles or chips of a contrasting color. You can enhance the natural look of these paths by letting the materials spill out into the landscape, but installing edging will reduce the need for maintenance.

# GRASS

day. Most grass species do not do well in shaded areas, although you may achieve some success with red fescues. In dry, arid climates, or where water supplies are scarce and regulated, it probably will not be practical to prepare and maintain a lawn path.

## DESIGN EFFECT/SITING

- Color and texture—Various shades of green, turning light brown when dormant. Textures vary from species to species, but the effect of texture generally diminishes over the area.
- Siting—Adaptable to both formal and informal styles—final effect depends on contours of path. Excellent for defining flower beds, borders, and shrubs.
- Grass allows subtle variations in color and texture with surrounding areas.

## ADVANTAGES

- Cut paths are the easiest and least expensive to construct. They also come with built-in borders—the precise edge left by the mower.
- Conforms readily to variations in terrain.
- Provides a soft, cool bed underfoot (less true of coarse-textured species).

## DISADVANTAGES

- Regular mowing, weeding, and watering can be demanding.
- Requires a waiting period—several weeks for seeded paths, somewhat shorter periods for sodded installations.
- Ungerminated seed and tilled soil may wash out in spring rains, especially on slopes.
- Frequent heavy traffic can create worn spots, especially with fine-textured species. A grass path to the children's play area, for example, may quickly turn into a dirt (or mud) path.

## DURABILITY AND MAINTENANCE

- Limited durability varies somewhat with the species and the amount of traffic.
- Success depends on matching species to climate (see "Warm- and Cool-Season Grasses"). Not recommended for arid regions or drought-prone areas.
- Responds well to natural freeze/thaw cycles.

Grass may seem an unusual choice for a path, but turf paths can solve many landscaping problems.

Gently curving and wide enough for two people, a lawn path can lead visitors informally from one planting bed to another. A narrow passage of grass can make a small garden seem larger. Lawn paths—sodded, seeded, or cut through taller grass—can transform a visually unenticing landscape into a place of natural beauty.

Although cut paths are easy to make, seeded paths require a little more work for soil preparation and planting. Sodding demands time and labor.

No matter what method you use, grass requires regular cutting, periodic fertilizing, and, in some areas, frequent watering.

Before you decide to use grass for your path, consider your climate and whether you want to devote the time necessary for the path's maintenance. Choose the grass suited to your region (see "Warm- and Cool-Season Grasses," opposite), and site your path so it gets several hours of direct sun each

## DESIGN TIPS

Use care when siting in shade, even filtered shade. Sites not receiving full shade may flourish at first but will need reseeding when they thin. Shade is not a constant. It increases as trees grow. Keep trees pruned to maintain a consistent amount of shade.

Experiment with the width of a grass path. Large flower beds may accommodate a wide path between them, but a grass path that is too wide will look like just more lawn. Start with a width not more than half the width of the largest planting bed.

**MAKING A GRASS PATH**

## HOW TO INSTALL

■ Send a soil sample to the local agricultural extension agent for testing. Add nutrients, lime, or other treatments as suggested.
■ Till and fertilize soil to a depth of 4–5 inches. For sodded surfaces, roll soil and lay sod strips. For seeding, rake tilled surface lightly, and seed. (See page 71 for instructions.)
■ Sod left on pallets more than 24 hours will begin to yellow and dry.

## HOW GRASS IS SOLD

■ Seed—in prepackaged bags or in bulk by the pound. Bulk seed costs less.
■ Sod (in 18- to 24-inch strips, 2 to 5 feet long)—by the pallet priced by the square yard or individual roll. Wider strips will save time and labor.

## ESTIMATING QUANTITIES

■ Determine the surface area of your path and order quantities to cover it.
■ Seed coverage varies. About 1½ pounds of Bermudagrass seed will cover a path 4 feet wide and 125 feet long. To seed the same path with fescue, you'll need twice as much seed.

Natural or wild area, or prairie-flower garden

Sod strips laid in tilled and rolled soil

Soil tilled 4–5", fertilized, and rolled

## WHERE TO BUY SEED AND SOD

■ You'll find bagged and bulk seed at garden centers, landscape outlets, home centers, and sometimes in hardware and grocery stores.
■ Garden centers and similar outlets often carry small quantities of sod, but you'll get a better price from a local sod farm—and a better chance of finding species compatible with your climate. Order sod in advance so the company can cut it before you need it.

## WARM- AND COOL-SEASON GRASSES

Not all grasses are alike. Although different species can be categorized botanically, what matters on a practical level is the climate in which a grass grows best. If you're planning a grass path, choose the species that will thrive in your climate. In general, grasses are either cool-season or warm-season species.

Cool-season grasses grow best in the northern United States, above an imaginary line (called the bluegrass line) that runs from east to west roughly from above North Carolina to Oklahoma to the Pacific Ocean. These grasses grow actively in cool spring weather and slow down or go dormant in the summer.

Most warm-season grasses don't thrive in cool climates and grow best in areas south of the bluegrass line and other regions with hot summers and mild winters. Warm-season grasses grow vigorously during the summer. Some go dormant in the winter; others won't survive the winter cold at all. Some grown in mild coastal climates will stay green all year.

■ **WARM-SEASON GRASSES**

| | | |
|---|---|---|
| Bermudagrass | Buffalograss | |
| St. Augustinegrass | Blue gramagrass (Buffalograss | |
| Zoysiagrass | and blue gramagrass will | |
| Bahiagrass | tolerate colder climates better | |
| Carpetgrass | than the other warm-weather | |
| Centipedegrass | species.) | |

■ **COOL-SEASON GRASSES**

Bentgrass
Kentucky bluegrass
Fine fescues
Tall fescues
Perennial ryegrass

# LOOSE STONE

Loose stone paths can bring more textures and colors into your landscape than any other material. Loose stone also adds an element not offered by other surfaces—sound. The subtle crunching of the material underfoot can be soothing as you amble along the path.

Loose stone is either rough or smooth. Rough materials, such as crushed granite chips or lava rock, tend to compact. Smooth stones, such as river rock or pea gravel, will also settle into the subbase, but their surface tends to migrate more with use.

You'll find many types, sizes, and colors of loose stone. Crushed quartz and quartz pebbles range from white to light pink. Crushed granite and lava rock are red. Dolomite and limestones are white or blue-gray. Pea gravel and river rock display a variety of colors. Larger river rock isn't as comfortable to walk on, but it can be an ornament or border for a path. For walking comfort, choose ¼- to ¾-inch aggregates.

## DESIGN EFFECT/SITING

■ Color and texture—Loose stone offers an endless array of colors and textures. Stone textures vary considerably, depending both on size and whether the stone is crushed or rounded mechanically or naturally.
■ Siting—Complements or contrasts both formal and informal designs. The final effect depends on contours of the path. Excellent for defining flower beds, borders, and shrubs.
■ Can provide dramatic contrasts to surrounding garden or lawn areas.

## ADVANTAGES

■ One of the least expensive materials for path construction; only slightly more expensive than organic materials.
■ Moderately easy to install.
■ Conforms to minor variations in terrain—crushed material holds well on gentle slopes.
■ Small stone can provide a flexible bed underfoot.
■ Drains quickly and is not subject to heaving in freeze/thaw cycles.
■ Cleans up easily—a light spray is usually enough to wash away dirt.

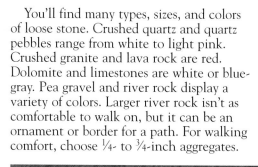

Crushed stone

Decomposed granite

Pea gravel

River stone

Quartz

Dolomite

Lava rock

## DESIGN TIPS

Put loose stone between the flower beds, or make a straight or formal ribbon through the yard. First pick the route, then the color and texture. Decide if you want the color to offset the predominant color scheme of your flower beds or complement it with a subtle change in hue. Some fine, crushed material will settle into the subbase and surrounding soil, creating a natural, borderless effect.

Choose colors carefully. Bluestone may look enticing in the bag, but too vivid when installed. White rock offers the starkest contrast and reflects the moonlight, but wide white walks may overwhelm a nearby flower bed. White rock also turns an unattractive gray over time.

## DISADVANTAGES

■ Stones over ¾ inch, although decorative, are not easy to walk on.
■ Moving wheeled equipment over it can be difficult.
■ Small smooth materials, such as pea gravel, can be displaced easily, making walking on slopes difficult.
■ Small materials may wash away on steep slopes.
■ Some stone, even crushed stone, is slippery if tracked onto a hard surface, such as a concrete patio.
■ White materials discolor easily.

## DURABILITY AND MAINTENANCE

■ Durability varies with traffic and the size of the aggregate. Heavy traffic can create worn spots that will require additional aggregate and raking to level.
■ Traffic may displace unbordered materials, and spillage may call for periodic raking.
■ Well suited to all climates. Proper drainage ensures reduced maintenance and durability.
■ Unaffected by freeze/thaw cycles.

## HOW TO INSTALL

■ Remove sod, and excavate to depth consistent with drainage requirements. Pour and level base material. Install edging and landscape fabric, then shovel or pour topping. (See illustration, below. Installation instructions are on page 72.)
■ Large stone covers a surface more quickly than smaller stone, but it is more difficult to spread.

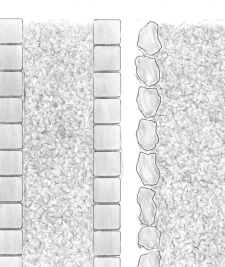

Loose stone with brick edging, alternate flat and edge-set

Loose stone with cut-stone edging

Loose stone with flagstone edging

## HOW LOOSE STONE IS SOLD

■ In bags by the cubic foot or in bulk (truckload) by the cubic yard or ton.

## ESTIMATING QUANTITIES

■ Determine the volume of your path and order quantities to cover it.

## WHERE TO BUY LOOSE STONE

■ You'll find bagged stone for small projects at garden centers, landscape outlets, home centers, and building supply stores.
■ Buying from a local quarry or sand and gravel yard will save money on a large project.

## MAKING A LOOSE STONE PATH

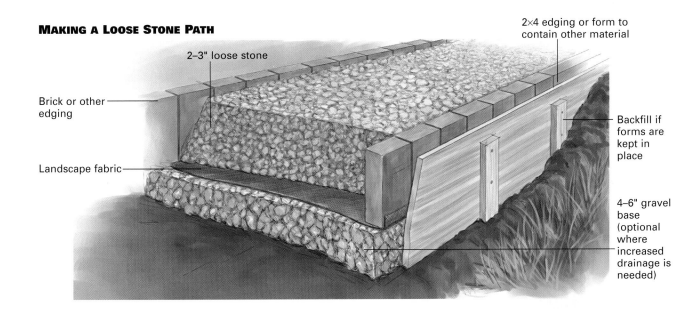

2×4 edging or form to contain other material

2–3" loose stone

Brick or other edging

Landscape fabric

Backfill if forms are kept in place

4–6" gravel base (optional where increased drainage is needed)

# FLAGSTONE

Limestone

Granite

Sandstone

River rubble

Slate

Quarry rubble

The general term *flagstone* refers to rock fractured or cleft into flat slabs 1 or 2 inches thick and used for paving.

Bluestone, limestone, redstone, sandstone, granite, and slate are usually used for building paths. Flagstone's irregular shape suits it to both free-form and geometric patterns—in individual stepping-stones or in stone surfaces set in sand or installed over a concrete base with mortar.

## DESIGN EFFECT/SITING

■ Color and texture—Flagstone offers an array of colors and textures. Colors range from gray-blue (bluestone) to various hues of tans and reds (limestone, granite, and sandstone), and deep, sometimes slightly iridescent blacks (slate). Textures vary from generally smooth to moderately rough.
■ Siting—Adaptable to both formal and informal styles; final effect depends on contours of the path. Stepping-stone paths almost always look casual. Sand-laid and mortared installations can enhance informal or formal styles, depending on their contours.
■ Random shapes and varied surface contours bring a sense of rustic, hand-hewn permanence to the landscape.

## ADVANTAGES

■ Stepping-stone and dry-set walks are among the easiest hard-surface materials to install. They require no specialized

## DESIGN TIPS

Use stepping-stones to slow down traffic so the viewer gets a better look at the surroundings. Stepping-stones fit meandering designs better than stone pavements.

To increase the formality of a design, keep straight edges to the outside of the path or use geometric edging, such as brick.

Use large stones to pave large expanses of landscape, smaller ones in smaller yards.

Lay out the general path contour on paper, then take the plans to the landscape to make sure your layout is practical and attractive. Design your flagstone walk on-site, laying out stepping-stones in a pleasing arrangement and experimenting with stone patterns to the side of the excavation.

skills. Mortared paths are more difficult.
■ Flagstone conforms moderately well to minor variations in terrain and works well on gentle slopes.
■ It adapts to an unlimited number of design variations.
■ Properly prepared, a flagstone path is not subject to heaving in freeze/thaw cycles, and it's virtually permanent.

## DISADVANTAGES

■ Large stones can be heavy, making them difficult to move and place.
■ A well-laid design will take time, especially if you're planning a stone surface set in sand or over concrete. Stepping-stone layouts require less precision.
■ It's more costly than loose stone.
■ Pores can collect water and become slick when frozen. Slate is slick when wet.

## DURABILITY AND MAINTENANCE

■ Most varieties will stand up to hard use, continued traffic, and wheeled garden equipment. Sandstone wears with use.
■ Stepping-stones may require periodic weeding, resetting, and leveling. Sand-laid stone may need occasional resetting.

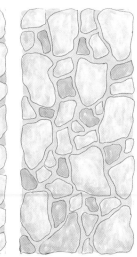

Equal sizes          Mixed sizes

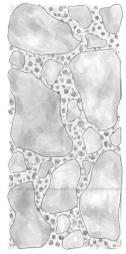

Mixed sizes with river rubble

Mortared walks need little maintenance.

■ Climate conditions have little effect on most flagstone varieties—they endure the harshest of conditions. Some porous rock, like sandstone, may absorb water and crack in freezing temperatures.

## HOW TO INSTALL

■ Remove sod, excavate consistent with drainage needs and material thickness. Install edging (optional) and landscape fabric; pour and level the base and sand bed. Lay out a trial pattern, then install the paving. Mortared installations require pouring a concrete slab and laying a mortar bed. (See illustrations below. Installation instructions are on page 74.)

■ Large stone will cover a surface more quickly than smaller stone, but it may prove harder to move, cut, and design.

## HOW FLAGSTONE IS SOLD

■ Suppliers usually sell it by the ton or square yard, although some will sell flagstone by the piece for small jobs. Order bulk on pallets to reduce breakage.

■ Prices vary with the size and type of stone. Stone native to your area will cost less.

## ESTIMATING QUANTITIES

■ Calculate square footage of your path. Your supplier will convert to tonnage, if necessary. One ton covers about 120 square feet.

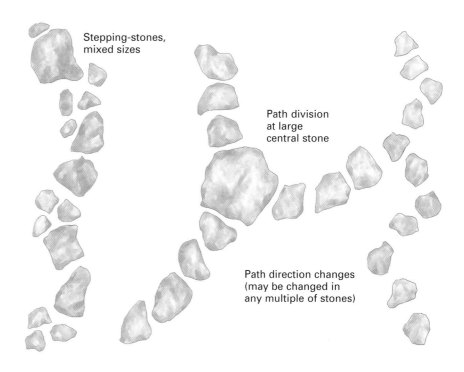

Stepping-stones, mixed sizes

Path division at large central stone

Path direction changes (may be changed in any multiple of stones)

## WHERE TO BUY FLAGSTONE

■ Garden centers, landscape outlets, home centers, and building supply retailers may carry individual pieces for small projects.

■ A bulk purchase from a local quarry or stone yard will save money on a large project. Handpicking your stone increases costs considerably.

## SAND-LAID FLAGSTONE INSTALLATION

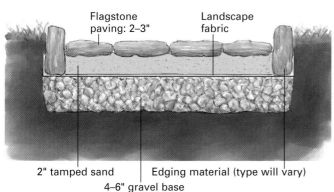

Flagstone paving: 2–3"

Landscape fabric

2" tamped sand

4–6" gravel base

Edging material (type will vary)

## MORTARED FLAGSTONE INSTALLATION

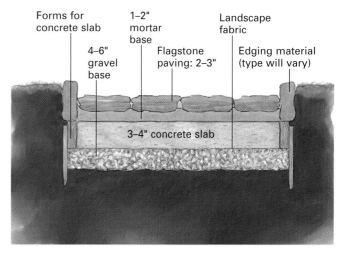

Forms for concrete slab

1–2" mortar base

Landscape fabric

4–6" gravel base

Flagstone paving: 2–3"

Edging material (type will vary)

3–4" concrete slab

# CUT STONE

Cut stone originates from the same natural rock as flagstone. The difference is in their shapes. Flagstone edges are natural and irregular. Cut stone is uniform, with straight edges and square corners. Cut-stone pieces range in size from about 1 to 4 feet and come in different thicknesses. Get paving at least 2 inches thick to avoid breakage under traffic.

This material lends itself to the same kind of installation as flagstone—as stepping-stones, in sand, or mortared to concrete. It is most often found set in sand for paths.

## DESIGN EFFECT/SITING

■ Color—You can choose from gray-blue (bluestone) to various hues of tans and reds (limestone, granite, and sandstone), to deep, sometimes slightly iridescent blacks (slate).

Marble comes in light-colored varieties, from yellow to pale white.
■ Texture—Most cut-stone surfaces are slightly rough. Marble is smooth.
■ Siting—It's used primarily in formal landscape designs, but can be cut and set into curves by skilled craftsmen.
■ The regularity of its geometric shapes adds a dignified, orderly flow to garden paths.

## ADVANTAGES

■ Installed as stepping-stones, cut stone requires only basic skills. Dry-set installations are only moderately harder to put in. Mortared paths are more difficult.
■ Small pieces conform well to minor variations in terrain.

## DESIGN TIPS

Although you can lay out the contours of the path on-site, it's best to design the actual pattern beforehand on paper.

Shop first, then design. Familiarizing yourself with the various shapes and sizes of cut stone will make it easier to plan the pattern. When you've decided on a pattern, lay out a section and measure its width.

To soften the formality of cut stone, bed it in brick, decorative tile, or loose stone. Leave a few pieces out of the pattern at random and plant those areas. Experiment with mixed sizes and diagonal axes.

Small stones may fall off the edges; put them in the center of the pattern. Avoid patterns that will form a cross in the joints. They will look like you've mistakenly broken the design.

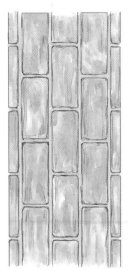

Equally sized stones set in offset bond

Equally sized stones set in parallel bond

Dissimilar stones set with joints parallel

■ Properly prepared, cut stone will withstand heaving in freeze/thaw cycles. Properly installed stone is practically permanent.

## DISADVANTAGES

■ It's more costly than flagstone.
■ Some varieties—slate and marble especially—can become slick when wet, which is dangerous on even moderate slopes.

## DURABILITY AND MAINTENANCE

■ Stepping-stones may require periodic weeding, resetting, and leveling. Sand-laid paths may need weeding, resanding, and resetting. Mortared walks need virtually no maintenance.
■ Most types of cut stone will stand up to hard use, continued traffic, and wheeled equipment. Soft stones, like sandstone, will wear away with use.
■ Climatic conditions don't affect most varieties. Sandstone, porous marble, and other porous rock may absorb water and crack in freezing temperatures.

## HOW TO INSTALL

■ Remove sod; excavate to depth consistent with drainage needs and material thickness. Install edging (optional) and landscape fabric. Pour and level base material and sand bed, then install paving. Mortared installations require pouring concrete and laying a mortar bed. (See illustrations below. Installation instructions are on page 78.)
■ Large stones will cover a surface quickly but are harder to move, cut, and design.

## HOW CUT STONE IS SOLD

■ Suppliers generally sell by the square foot or square yard, rarely by the piece. Order bulk on pallets to reduce breakage.

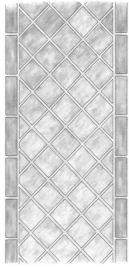
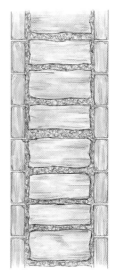

Alternate squares in loose stone     Diagonal setting     Parallel stone set in gravel

■ Prices vary with the size, type, and color. Stone native to your area will cost less.

## ESTIMATING QUANTITIES

■ Determine the square footage of your path. If you're using similar-sized stones, divide the area of the path by the average area of a stone. For designs using different stone sizes, figure the average number of pieces of each size per square foot, then multiply the quantity for each size by the area of the path that will be covered by that size. A design using different sizes will cost more.

## WHERE TO BUY FLAGSTONE

■ Purchase from a local masonry supplier, stone yard, or tile outlet. Contact a stonemason if you can't find a local source.

### SAND-LAID CUT-STONE INSTALLATION

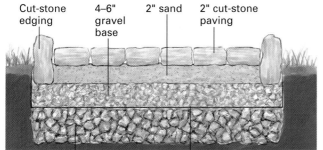

Cut-stone edging    4–6" gravel base    2" sand    2" cut-stone paving

4–6"crushed stone (optional for increased drainage)    Landscape fabric (Put landscape fabric on top of gravel if not using crushed-stone base.)

### MORTARED CUT-STONE INSTALLATION

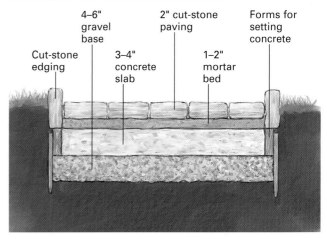

4–6" gravel base    2" cut-stone paving    Forms for setting concrete

Cut-stone edging    3–4" concrete slab    1–2" mortar bed

# BRICK AND CONCRETE PAVERS

**Pavers**    **Manufactured salvage brick**    **Common brick**    **Used brick**    **Adobe pavers**

If you're looking for a warm, earthy material that lends an old-world formality to your path, brick is the best choice.

Most distributors stock a wide variety of sizes, colors, styles, and densities. And if you purchase a modular style—meaning the dimensions are proportional—design becomes virtually goof-proof.

When shopping for materials, avoid common brick, face brick, and firebrick. These varieties are not made for paving. Look for any of these types:

■ Paving brick. It resists moisture and wear. Some types have rounded or chamfered edges, which makes it easier to install in a sand base.

■ Brick salvaged from old buildings or streets. These may come with the mortar left on; many designers believe this adds to the charm of a cottage path.

Depending on its original use, used brick may be softer than paving brick and may not wear as well. Many homeowners find its worn appearance enhances its rustic look. You can approximate a used-brick look with manufactured salvage brick.

Brick is graded for hardness. The SX grade withstands the most severe weather conditions and costs more. If you live in northern climates, the extra cost may be worthwhile. In milder climates, MX grade holds up to light frosts. Your supplier will be able to help you decide.

■ Adobe pavers. Impregnated with asphalt, they resist water almost as well as clay brick. They are not fired at high temperatures, however, so they won't stand up to hard use. Install them in sand in dry climates not prone to freezing.

## DESIGN EFFECT/SITING

■ Color—Colors range from white and light yellow through reds and dark browns.
■ Texture—Paving is slightly rough, but the effect of texture depends more on the pattern and installation method than on the brick.
■ Siting—Used primarily in formal landscape designs, but can be cut and laid in gentle or dramatic shapes. Its modular dimensions fit almost any design.

## ADVANTAGES

■ Modular bricks are easy to lay in sand, requiring only basic skills and a little time. Mortared paths are more difficult.
■ Conforms well to minor terrain variations.
■ Fits an endless array of designs. Mixes well with other materials. Excellent for edging.
■ Properly set, brick is permanent.

**Running bond**

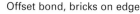

**Offset bond, bricks on edge**

**Diagonal bond**

Basket weave

45° herringbone

90° herringbone

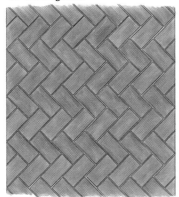

## DISADVANTAGES

■ Salvaged brick may crack in winter and gradually crumble in any season.
■ Moss can grow on brick when damp. Smooth brick surfaces can become slick when wet, posing a danger on even moderate slopes.

## DESIGN TIPS

You can use brick in a wide variety of designs. The illustrations on these pages show a few of the possibilities. Consider using brick for the front walk, for paths that wind through a kitchen garden or orchard, or for edging a flagstone walk that meanders toward a backyard bench.

When you've decided on a preliminary pattern for your brick path, lay out a section and measure its width. Don't forget to include the width of the mortar joints if you will set a mortared path. Adjust the actual width on your plan to the total width of the pattern. (See illustration on page 46 for more information.)

Add interest to your brick design with alternating colors. Slight contrasts—a red-brown interspersed with dark red bricks, for example—look more pleasing than sharply contrasting colors. Bricks set on edge offer unusual design possibilities, but the smaller edge surface will require more bricks and a larger budget for your path.

Consider safety, too, when shopping for brick; don't use bricks with slick surfaces.

## DURABILITY AND MAINTENANCE

■ New pavers stand up to hard use, continued traffic, and wheeled garden equipment. Used brick wears away with use.
■ Brick set in sand may require periodic weeding, resetting, and leveling. Mortared walkways need virtually no maintenance.
■ Most brick will stand up to weather if properly bedded. Some porous brick may absorb water and crack when it freezes.

### SAND-LAID BRICK INSTALLATION

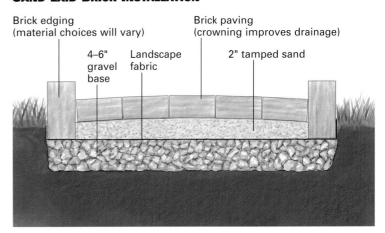

Brick edging
(material choices will vary)

4–6"
gravel
base

Landscape
fabric

Brick paving
(crowning improves drainage)

2" tamped sand

### MORTARED-BRICK INSTALLATION

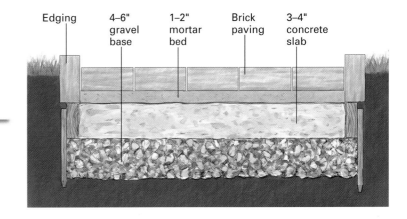

Edging

4–6"
gravel
base

1–2"
mortar
bed

Brick
paving

3–4"
concrete
slab

# BRICK AND CONCRETE PAVERS
*continued*

## HOW TO INSTALL

■ Remove existing sod and excavate. Install edging (optional) and landscape fabric. Pour and level base material and sand bed. Install paving. Mortared installations require pouring a concrete slab and laying a mortar bed. (See the illustrations on page 35. Installation instructions are on page 80.)

## HOW BRICK IS SOLD

■ Brick is sold individually or in square yards. Order on pallets to reduce breakage.
■ Prices vary with the size, type, and color.

## ESTIMATING QUANTITIES

■ Determine the area of your path in square feet. Multiply the path area by five. (About five standard 2×4×8-inch bricks cover 1 square foot.) Order 5 to 10 percent extra to allow for cutting and breakage. For other brick sizes, divide the path area by the face area of one brick.

## WHERE TO BUY BRICK

■ Purchase brick from brickyards, lumberyards, or garden and home centers. Most will deliver for a small fee.
■ Some specialty-brick suppliers maintain Internet websites.

## CONCRETE PAVERS

Concrete pavers resemble brick in their versatility and installation. Once made only as gray squares, they are now manufactured in a variety of shapes and colors. In fact, rectangular pavers are used less now than other shapes—circles, chamfered squares, diamonds, hexagons, octagons, crescents, and more.

Textures also abound—from smooth to stamped to aggregate surfaces. Colors come in a narrow range, typically reminiscent of brick—reds, browns, and tan earth tones—but also in blacks, grays, and off-whites. Some pavers look remarkably like brick, stone, adobe, marble, or cobblestone. Look carefully at the depth of the color, and avoid pavers with color that looks shallow. Colors applied just to the surface can wear off quickly.

Concrete pavers are manufactured from dense, pressure-formed, cast concrete. They are cured, unlike bricks, which are made from fired clay.

They are as durable as brick, but lighter in weight and less costly. Many are thinner, too, starting at about 1½ inches and running up to the size of brick—2½ inches—and larger. You'll find large rectangles about 4×6 inches (and up to about 9 inches), geometrics about 2×4 inches, and keyed varieties that you can lay in circles and fans.

## DESIGN TIPS

Because of their regularity, many concrete pavers look best in formal design schemes. The paver itself creates the pattern.

Pay close attention to the scale when you make your dimensioned plan. A small paver can make any path look busy. Large pavers take less time to set because each unit covers more area, but don't let their size overwhelm the width of your installation.

In the planning stages, if you sense that your design will look too busy, use larger pavers or consider spacing them farther apart. You can reduce the busy look by planting in the gaps.

Concrete pavers come in different categories, based on how they are designed to be installed:

■ Interlocking pavers resist lateral movement because their sides—contoured, more than four sided, S-shaped, or crescents—fit together to keep the units stable. They'll stay in place even under heavy use and dramatic changes in the weather. Manufactured corner and end pieces don't need cutting.

■ Standard pavers are rectangular and not as stable as the interlocking variety. They may shift over time, especially if your pathway gets hard use or is set in poorly draining soil.

■ Turf blocks have an open design with recesses intended for planting. They are even strong enough to be used in driveways.

All varieties are weatherproof and extremely durable.

## HOW TO INSTALL

Install concrete pavers in sand or a mortar bed using the same techniques as you would for brick. Sand-bed installations are more common. Some pavers are molded with built-in tabs that give you consistent spacing in sand-laid installations. (Installation instructions are on page 84.)

## ESTIMATING QUANTITIES

Calculate the area of your path and divide it by the coverage of the particular paver style recommended by the manufacturer or distributor.

## WHERE TO BUY CONCRETE PAVERS

Building supply centers, concrete suppliers, landscape centers, and home and garden centers sell concrete pavers individually, by the square foot, or in banded cubes (enough for about 16 linear feet).

## MAKE YOUR OWN

You can make your own pavers with ready-mix concrete and homemade or manufactured forms. Round or rectangular shapes are easiest to make in homemade forms. Garden and home centers sell a wider variety of shapes and sizes. (See page 91 for more information.)

## TILING A PATH

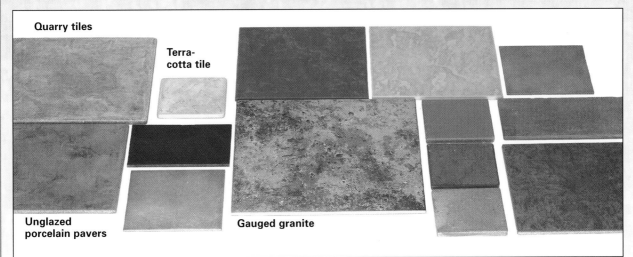

Quarry tiles

Terra-cotta tile

Unglazed porcelain pavers

Gauged granite

With its regular geometric shapes and distinct edges, ceramic and stone tile makes an excellent paving choice for formal designs. For outdoor use in cold climates, install tile that doesn't absorb water.

Unglazed quarry tile (red-bodied and about ⅜ inch thick), unglazed pavers (porcelain and other nonvitreous clays), and gauged stone tile (slate, marble, and granite ground to a uniform thickness) are the common types. Homeowners on a budget should consider synthetic stone tiles—clay tile stained to look like stone.

Climate conditions in your region will probably dictate what kind of tile local distributors carry.

Like brick, the uniform size of the tile you use means the width of the path has to be equal to the width of the pattern. Measure a trial section of your pattern and plan the path to fit. This avoids cutting tile to fit. If cuts are necessary—to fit at the edge of a stairs or patio, for example—rent a snap cutter. Snap-cutting is an easy process. The rental outlet staff can show you how to do it in a matter of minutes.

Installation methods are the same as mortared brick.

**Railway ties**

**Treated 4×4 landscape timber**

**Treated 2×6 decking**

**Redwood decking**

# WOOD

Wood lends a warmth to the landscape that no other material can match. Its appealing, organic look offers numerous design options. You can set it directly in the soil, in a sand bed, or in anchored frames.

Insects, rot, and mildew attack most woods. Redwood, cypress, and cedar, however, contain natural resins that resist insects and the elements. Get the heartwood only of these species—the sapwood is not resistant. Tropical hardwoods are durable and their initial high cost can be worth the years of freedom from maintenance. Look for tropical woods from sustainable-forestry sources.

Pressure-treated lumber offers a less expensive alternative to resistant species. Treated wood is infused with chemicals (including arsenic, which will be phased out during 2003) that greatly reduce its susceptibility to rot and insects. Treatment compounds turn the wood green or tan, but the color weathers to a gray within several months. You can stain treated and untreated lumber to any color.

Buy treated lumber rated for ground contact. Look for a *Ground Contact* or *LP25* stamp (or both) on the surface of the wood. Read the safety label attached to the lumber, and follow the instructions. Wear gloves when handling treated wood and a respirator or dust mask when sawing it.

When shopping, inspect each piece. Don't buy split, cupped, or twisted pieces. Small knots are acceptable, but large knots may work their way out or cause the lumber to split—especially near an edge. Slight bowing will flatten when fastened in place.

## DESIGN EFFECT/SITING

■ Color—Natural colors range from light (cypress) to purple-red (cedar) to redwood's deep reddish-brown. The green cast of treated lumber turns gray in time. Stains, paints, and finishes will alter colors to suit your taste.
■ Texture—Generally smooth but conveyed more by pattern and design than by the material itself.
■ Siting—Wood will almost always look informal in the landscape, but it is suitable for formal, rectangular designs, especially as edging and in modular designs.

## ADVANTAGES

■ Wood is less expensive than brick, flagstone, and cut stone (though more expensive than loose stone and organic materials).
■ Ease of installation depends on complexity of design, but generally requires only basic carpentry skills.
■ Wood mixes well with other materials.

## DISADVANTAGES

■ Can become moss-covered when damp.

## DESIGN TIPS

Wood can go almost anywhere, but it is especially suited to woodland paths, boardwalks, and footbridges. It makes stylish decked walkways.

Cut your own wood rounds with a chain saw. Embed them (or 3- to 4-inch lengths of timber set on edge) in loose stone or sand. Plant groundcovers in the spaces or fill the gaps with bark.

**INSTALLING DECKING ON SLEEPERS**

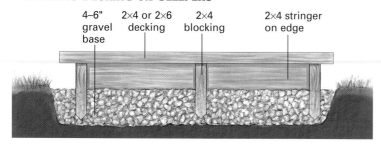

4–6" gravel base | 2×4 or 2×6 decking | 2×4 blocking | 2×4 stringer on edge

2×4 decking on sleepers

Diagonal 2×4s on cross frame

2×4s on sleepers in staggered sections

Perpendicular 2×4s on sleepers

Landscape timbers set in loose stone

Surfaces get slick when wet, which can be dangerous on slopes and steps.
■ Does not conform as well to terrain variations. Changes in slope require posts or installation of small sections.

## DURABILITY AND MAINTENANCE

■ You will have to occasionally replace worn or damaged decking and reapply finishes and preservatives, even in mild-weather installations.

## HOW TO INSTALL

■ Remove sod, excavate, and install wood rounds or sections. For boardwalks, set posts or sleepers, then install decking. (See illustrations at right. Installation instructions are on page 86.)

## HOW WOOD IS SOLD

■ Wood is sold by the piece or by the board foot. Prices vary with the size and species.

## ESTIMATING QUANTITIES

■ Determine square footage and structural requirements. Take your dimensioned plan to your supplier for assistance.

## WHERE TO BUY WOOD

■ Purchase wood from lumberyards or home centers.

## CONSTRUCTING A BOARDWALK

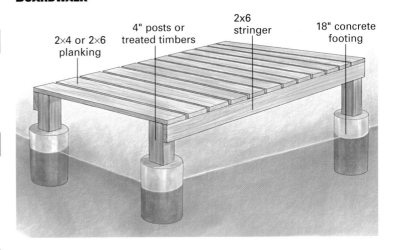

2×4 or 2×6 planking

4" posts or treated timbers

2x6 stringer

18" concrete footing

## EMBEDDING WOOD ROUNDS AND BLOCKS

Crosscut wood block

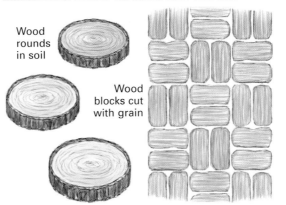

Wood rounds in soil

Wood blocks cut with grain

# POURED CONCRETE

Because concrete installs as a liquid and cures to a hard, durable solid, it adapts easily to any design. You can pour it in gentle, meandering curves or in straight, formal configurations. Modern concrete techniques—such as stamping, coloring, texturing, and embedding with aggregates—can create a dazzling path or driveway surface.

*Poured concrete doesn't have to be flat and gray. Concrete can be colored and textured (above and at right). Stamped patterns, such as the brick effect below, and stenciled designs can make concrete look like other paving materials.*

## DESIGN EFFECT/SITING

- Color—Gray in its natural state, but any color can be added.
- Texture—Smooth or moderately rough when unfinished. Stamping, aggregates, and texturing can mimic other materials.
- Siting—Can be sited anywhere and in any design scheme.

## ADVANTAGES

- Unlimited design potential.
- Requires little maintenance.

## DISADVANTAGES

- Requires careful planning and, on large projects, some heavy equipment.
- Installation is hard work and requires careful preparation. Large projects require helpers.
- Concrete has to be worked within specified time limits.

## DURABILITY AND MAINTENANCE

- Stands up to all climatic conditions.
- Resists damage from freeze/thaw cycles if properly installed.
- Gets hot in direct sunlight and can be cold and slick in winter.
- If necessary, order additive in the mix to accommodate hot or cold temperatures while curing.
- Extremely durable if properly mixed and poured.

## HOW TO INSTALL

- Remove sod, then excavate. Install forms, pour, and finish. (See illustration, opposite. Installation instructions are on page 88.)

## HOW CONCRETE IS SOLD

- Ingredients (portland cement, sand, and aggregate) are available separately or pre-mixed in bags. Concrete delivered by a mixing truck is sold by the cubic yard.

## ESTIMATING QUANTITIES

- Determine the volume of your path, and add 5 percent.
- A 40-pound bag of pre-mix makes $\frac{1}{3}$ cubic foot; a 60-pound bag, $\frac{1}{2}$ cubic foot; and an 80-pound bag, $\frac{2}{3}$ cubic foot.

1" aggregate with broken-brick edging

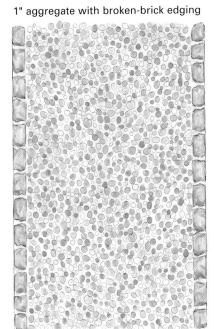

1" aggregate embedded in squares

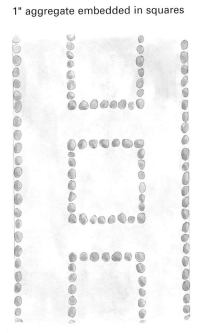

River rubble and broken brick

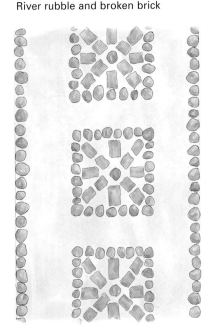

A 4×20-foot walk 4 inches deep requires 26⅔ cubic feet of concrete—about 1 cubic yard (27 cubic feet).

## WHERE TO BUY CONCRETE

■ Buy pre-mix at a hardware store, home center, lumberyard, or building supply center.
■ Order bulk concrete from a ready-mix concrete company.

## WHAT ABOUT ASPHALT?

If you're looking for an inexpensive alternative to concrete paving, asphalt might fill the bill. But don't try to do the job yourself. Asphalt installation requires heavy equipment and is a job best done by a paving contractor.

Also called blacktop or macadam, asphalt is a mix of sand, gravel, and petroleum. It has many of the same qualities as concrete. It pours as a liquid, sets to a solid, and can be stamped and colored to resemble brick and stone.

You can pour, level, and roll another product called cold-rolled asphalt. It's sold by the bag at home centers—an inexpensive alternative if you're just topping off an existing slab that's in good condition.

## INSTALLING A POURED-CONCRETE PATH

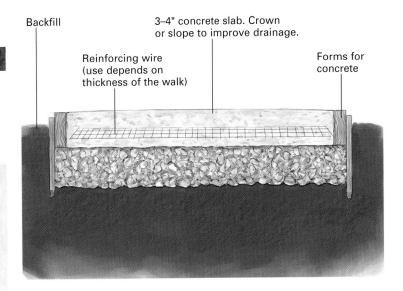

Backfill

3–4" concrete slab. Crown or slope to improve drainage.

Reinforcing wire (use depends on thickness of the walk)

Forms for concrete

## DESIGN TIPS

You can easily plan concrete projects on paper—concrete will conform to any contour and width. Include the stamped pattern or aggregate design on your plan to get a sense of proper scale. With such detail, even the sidewalk that leads to the trash containers will look attractive. Include all the details on paper before pouring; you won't be able to make changes after you start.

# AROUND THE EDGES

Edgings do more than contain path materials. They become part of the design. Edging not only defines the contour of the path, it can add complementary or contrasting colors and textures to your design.

The most common edging materials are described on these pages, but you can use practically anything you desire. River stone, whole or broken shells, broken brick or block—even reclaimed roofing tiles— also make attractive and functional edging.

### BRICKS

Brick soldiers (set upright and on edge) and sailors (set flat along the edge of the path) enhance both formal and informal designs. So do bricks set on an angle on edge. Although its modular form lends itself to formal designs, brick works as an edge for informal paths as well. Set brick in a gravel and sand base or in a concrete footing for increased stability.

### BRICK EDGING

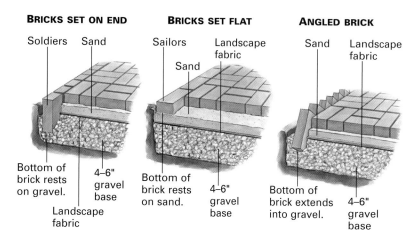

**BRICKS SET ON END**
Soldiers  Sand
Bottom of brick rests on gravel.
4–6" gravel base
Landscape fabric

**BRICKS SET FLAT**
Sailors  Landscape fabric
Sand
Bottom of brick rests on sand.
4–6" gravel base

**ANGLED BRICK**
Sand  Landscape fabric
Bottom of brick extends into gravel.
4–6" gravel base

### POURED CONCRETE

Poured concrete, the strongest of edging materials, can be colored during mixing to match or contrast with the path material. Texture poured concrete edging with any of the techniques shown on pages 90–91.

### CONCRETE EDGING

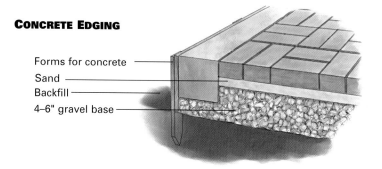

Forms for concrete
Sand
Backfill
4–6" gravel base

### PLASTIC AND STEEL

Flexible plastic edging will conform to almost any curve. It's easy to install by anchoring it to the ground with spikes driven through integral lugs.

Use steel edging to contain concrete and other heavy materials. Buy ¼-inch commercial-grade steel for maximum stability. Both plastic and steel edgings should be buried below the edge of the surface materials so they will not show.

### MOLDED PLASTIC EDGING

Spikes anchor edging into gravel bed and soil.

4–6" gravel base

Concrete

### WOOD/ LANDSCAPE TIMBERS

Wood (2×4s, 2×6s, or 2×8s), landscape timbers (4×4s or 8×8s), and other lumber bring a pleasant contrast to brick or concrete paths. Be sure to use naturally resistant species or pressure-treated stock rated for ground contact. Stake lumber

## WOOD/LANDSCAPE-TIMBER EDGING

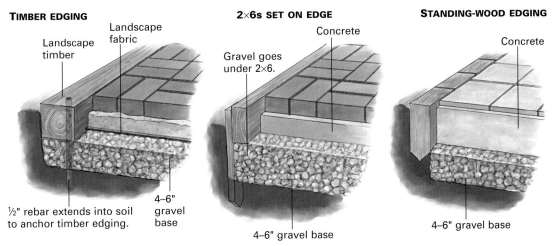

**TIMBER EDGING**

Landscape timber

Landscape fabric

½" rebar extends into soil to anchor timber edging.

4–6" gravel base

**2×6s SET ON EDGE**

Concrete

Gravel goes under 2×6.

4–6" gravel base

**STANDING-WOOD EDGING**

Concrete

4–6" gravel base

in place with the stakes below the top edge. Backfill with topsoil to hide the stakes. If you're setting timbers, predrill them every 3 feet and drive a ½-inch rebar through the holes into the soil.

## STONE

Both flagstone and cut stone make excellent edging, especially for wide walks. You can purchase precut stone or cut the pieces yourself from paving stones. When cutting your own, make sure you keep the width consistent so the stones don't look mismatched.

## PRECAST EDGING

Precast pavers or tiles are made by many manufacturers to match your paver pattern. They come in straight or curved shapes, many with sculpted designs. You can also use precast blocks by themselves as borders for planting beds.

### STONE EDGING

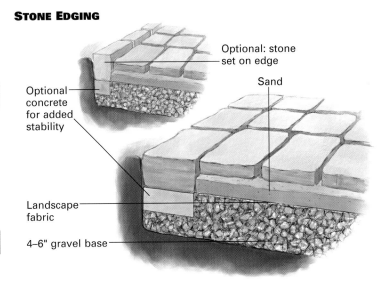

Optional: stone set on edge

Sand

Optional concrete for added stability

Landscape fabric

4–6" gravel base

### PRECAST EDGING

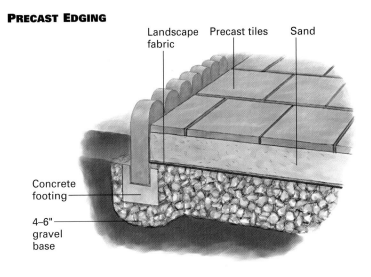

Landscape fabric

Precast tiles

Sand

Concrete footing

4–6" gravel base

## INSTALLATION TIPS

Loose materials, such as bark and stone, need edging to keep them in the path. Hard surfaces set in sand also need edging to keep the paving in place.

For most paths, install the edging before the paving materials. That way you can use the edging to help level the surface. Set separate edging for a concrete path after the slab is cured.

Setting the edging slightly below the lawn surface will make mowing neat and easy.

*Begin your landscape plan by making a dimensioned sketch of your property, as shown at right. Working from the sketch, draw a scaled plan on graph paper, shown on the opposite page. Stick-on landscape symbols, such as the trees shown, are available at art supply stores. Sketch your paths and other planned features on the scaled plan.*

## SHOULD I HIRE A PRO?

The rapid growth of the do-it-yourself industry shows that many homeowners are willing to tackle all but the most extensive landscaping projects. Use this checklist to help decide whether to do the work yourself or contract it.

■ Weigh your skills against the demands of the project. You can excavate almost any path you design, but if the site is large, hiring an excavating contractor might make more sense.

■ Two sets of hands (or more) will lighten the load. Enlist the help of friends who have the skills you don't. A crew of friends also makes the job more enjoyable.

■ When you're figuring your costs, include everything— materials, supplies, the cost of new and rented tools, and debris removal. Compare your total with bids you solicit. Doing the job yourself can save you from one-third to one-half the cost of a contracted project. But if you're short on time or skills, the cost might be worth it.

■ If you decide to contract the work, get references from friends before you start. Avoid bids that are significantly higher or lower than the average. Look at the contract carefully. Good contracts contain details—materials lists, timelines, insurance information, and protection from liens placed by subcontractors if the contractor doesn't pay them.

## HIGH-TECH PLANNING

If you're planning to remake your entire landscape design scheme, computer landscape-design software can make the job much easier. The programs are easy to use and flexible, and can speed your progress from base plan to final design. You'll find them especially useful when making changes; you can alter your plans without having to redraw them.

The programs will do everything— calculate dimensions of each structure, create side elevations and three-dimensional views, make material lists, and make patterns on your walkway. They'll even put trees and shrubs where you want them.

Recent home improvement and gardening magazines will carry reviews of the newest programs. Check with your home improvement or building supply center. More and more of these retail outlets offer computer design services at no cost if you purchase your materials from them.

# PUTTING YOUR PATH ON PAPER

All paths require planning. Even if you are only building a short walk from the house to the garage or garden shed, the project will go more smoothly if you first put the path on paper.

Drawing the path first saves you from having to make hurried decisions while building it. It allows you to experiment with the location of the path, its contours, and the pattern of its materials. Paper plans can also give you a bird's-eye view of the landscape, helping you discover design ideas you might not otherwise have seen.

The planning steps shown in this chapter are helpful when planning a complete landscape design too. Even if the only alteration you plan to make in your yard is a path to the kitchen garden, it will still help to sketch the layout to scale on graph paper. Scaled drawings also help you plan future improvements to your yard so your present project won't interfere with the landscape you ultimately want to achieve.

Although there are no rigid rules to tell you how to design your landscape, the best plans contain some logic. They incorporate new elements into the existing design, fitting them appropriately to the space available and reflecting the intended uses. Take a few hours or several days when you make your master plan. Experimenting on paper can save you hours of frustration in the long run.

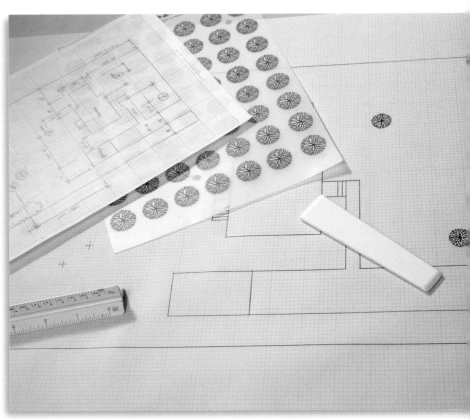

# DEVELOPING YOUR MASTER PLAN

Developing your master plan involves four different steps. Each step requires a scaled drawing on graph paper. Graph paper with a ¼-inch scale (¼ inch = 1 foot) makes the job easy.

**BASE MAP:** First make a base map— a scaled drawing of your property that includes property lines and major existing features, such as the house, outbuildings, and trees.

If you're just putting in a simple path and not making any major alterations to the landscape, you can limit your drawing to the path itself, including its starting and end points (see illustration below).

Even if you're adding only one or two new elements to your landscape, a base map is a good place to start. You can sketch out the locations of your new path and minor improvements right on the base map, as in the illustration below. Be sure they're drawn to scale, however.

**SITE ANALYSIS:** More involved landscape alterations call for a full-scale base map and a site analysis. The site analysis is the map of your yard with notations indicating problem areas, changes that need to be made, views and elements you want to keep, and the location of microclimates and harsh weather conditions.

**BUBBLE PLANS AND CONCEPT DIAGRAMS:** These drawings, shown on page 48, chart the uses of your yard and the elements you want to install for those purposes. Show rough indications of what features go where on these diagrams.

**MASTER PLAN:** All of this work will appear on your master plan, which will detail the new additions to your landscape—from paths to pergolas, planting beds to decks.

## MAKING A BASE MAP

The easiest way to create a base map is to make a scaled copy of your plat map, which may be among the papers from closing the purchase of your home. You can also get a copy from your local tax assessor or county recorder.

Take measurements of your yard and transfer them to the base map on your graph paper. Take a sketch of the house, a clipboard, and a 100-foot steel tape measure to the yard to draw the plan. Include these elements:

**BASE MAP, NEW PATH ONLY**

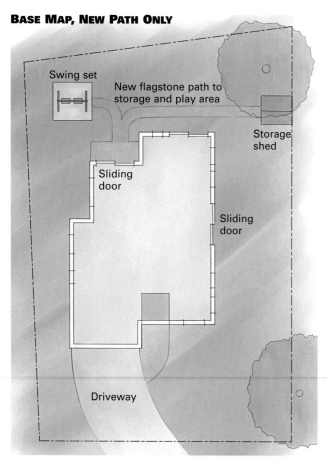

**BASE MAP, NEW PATH AND PLANTING BEDS**

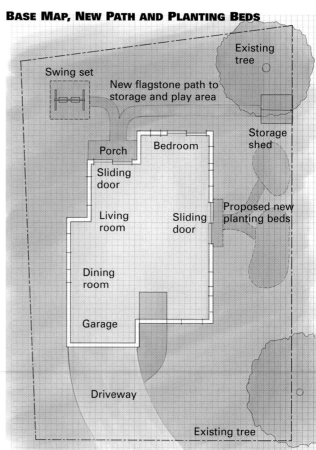

- The distance of major elements—trees, the house, garden shed, a detached garage, and others—from the property lines and from each other.
- Location of doors and windows and the rooms to which they lead.
- The extension of roof eaves beyond the walls of the house (if you are building a new deck or patio).
- Downspouts and the direction of runoff.
- The direction and pitch of slopes or major differences in ground levels.

## ANALYZING YOUR SITE

Once you've completed the base map, list the assets (things you want to keep) and liabilities (things you want to change). A thorough site analysis should include:
- Views you want to maintain or hide.
- Nearby sources of noise, both day and night.
- Elements to increase privacy.
- Drainage that needs correction.
- Grading that needs to be done to improve the use of your property.
- Direction of prevailing winds.
- Sun and shade patterns.
- Natural traffic patterns.

## KEEPING THINGS ORGANIZED

Landscape projects progress in a natural order. Make a written work schedule with timelines to coordinate all the aspects of your landscape makeover.
- Prepare the site—remove unwanted trees and shrubs, and mark any plantings you intend to save.
- Excavate—dig out the area of your path, as well as any footings required for new construction.
- Pour concrete, if required.
- Lay path and paving materials.
- Rough carpentry—build decks, fences, and sheds.
- Electrify the landscape—install wiring and circuit breakers.
- Finish up—complete the finish carpentry, stain and paint, and sod or seed new lawns and plantings.

### TYPICAL SITE ANALYSIS

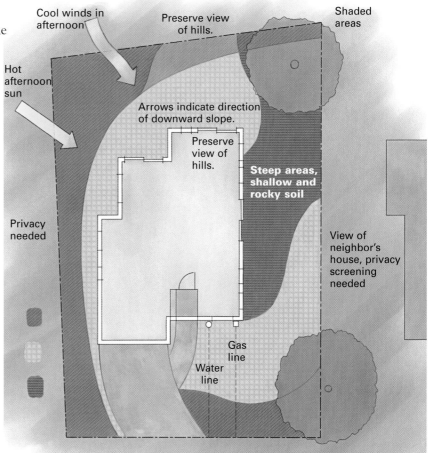

Cool winds in afternoon
Preserve view of hills.
Shaded areas
Hot afternoon sun
Arrows indicate direction of downward slope.
Preserve view of hills.
Steep areas, shallow and rocky soil
Privacy needed
View of neighbor's house, privacy screening needed
Gas line
Water line

## DESIGNING DRIVEWAYS

Driveways are often last on the design list because they are seen as purely functional. But driveways can be beautiful too.

The illustration at right shows minimum dimensions for new drives. If your drive doesn't measure up, don't tear it up. Instead add areas for parking, and increase spaces where people get out of the car.

A new surface on the driveway can change the character of the front of your home. So can new pathways. Use the existing crushed-rock drive as the foundation for a slab stamped in a stone pattern. Build a brick path from the slab to the front door. The contrast will call attention to the walk and the house.

Redesigning edging and screening parking areas with plants can make an old driveway look new.

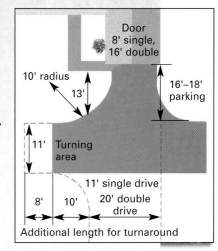

Door 8' single, 16' double
10' radius
13'
16'–18' parking
11' Turning area
11' single drive
8' | 10' | 20' double drive
Additional length for turnaround

# DEVELOPING YOUR MASTER PLAN
*continued*

## TYPICAL BUBBLE PLAN

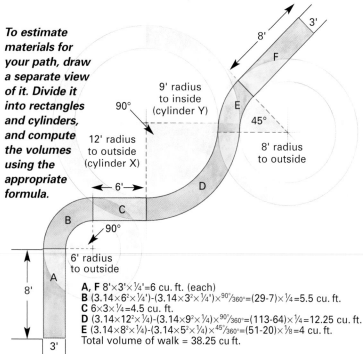

## TYPICAL CONCEPT DIAGRAM

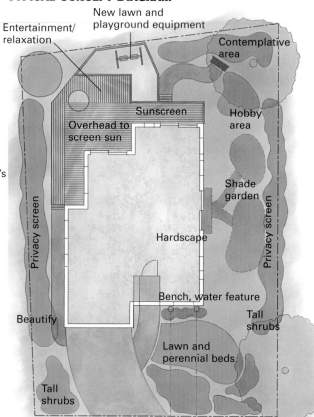

## COMPUTING VOLUME OF REGULAR AND IRREGULAR SHAPES

### CYLINDRICAL SOLID

Volume = π (3.14) × radius² × depth
(Use same units—inches or feet—
for radius (r) and depth.)

### RECTANGULAR SOLID

Volume = length × width × depth
(Use same units—inches or feet—
for length, width, and depth.)

The depth of the path in
the example is 3", or ¼'.

Volume of walkway curve (shaded area) =
[Volume of cylinder X] – [volume of cylinder Y] × [arc of curve / 360°]

*To estimate
materials for
your path, draw
a separate view
of it. Divide it
into rectangles
and cylinders,
and compute
the volumes
using the
appropriate
formula.*

9' radius
to inside
(cylinder Y)

90°

12' radius
to outside
(cylinder X)

45°

8' radius
to outside

8' radius
to outside

6'

90°

6' radius
to outside

3'

8'

**A, F** 8'×3'×¼'=6 cu. ft. (each)
**B** (3.14×6²×¼')-(3.14×3²×¼')×⁹⁰°/₃₆₀°=(29-7)×¼=5.5 cu. ft.
**C** 6×3×¼=4.5 cu. ft.
**D** (3.14×12²×¼)-(3.14×9²×¼)×⁹⁰°/₃₆₀°=(113-64)×¼=12.25 cu. ft.
**E** (3.14×8²×¼)-(3.14×5²×¼)×⁴⁵°/₃₆₀°=(51-20)×⅛=4 cu. ft.
Total volume of walk = 38.25 cu ft.

## MAKING A BUBBLE PLAN

A bubble plan lets you dream and experiment on paper.

Tape a piece of tracing paper on your site analysis and draw quick circles that represent how you want to use areas in your yard. Let each circle represent an area defined by use— not by the particular element that goes in it.

Label each area with its intended use. Be general, not specific. Experiment with different layouts and labels.

If you don't like one plan, tape another sheet of tracing paper on and draw different bubbles. This is the time for making changes, not after you've begun the project itself.

## FROM BUBBLES TO CONCEPTS

A concept diagram is a refinement of your bubble plan. Here you begin to specify— still in a general way—the elements you want in each area.

On your final bubble plan, jot simple notes that describe any addition to an area within a bubble. Be general. For example, in the concept diagram above, the entertainment area is labeled *hard scape*. You can decide later whether it will be a deck or a flagstone patio.

Connect the bubbles with arrows to show traffic patterns. And if something doesn't

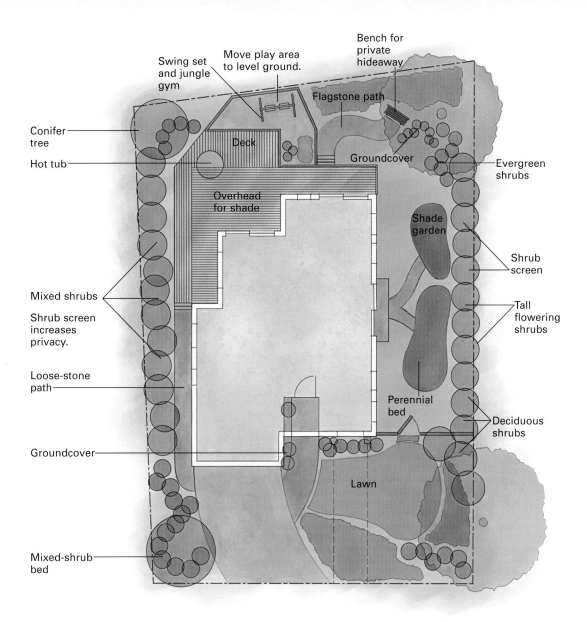

Swing set and jungle gym

Move play area to level ground.

Bench for private hideaway

Flagstone path

Conifer tree

Hot tub

Deck

Overhead for shade

Groundcover

Evergreen shrubs

Shade garden

Shrub screen

Mixed shrubs

Shrub screen increases privacy.

Tall flowering shrubs

Loose-stone path

Perennial bed

Deciduous shrubs

Groundcover

Lawn

Mixed-shrub bed

work, tape a clean piece of paper on and refine your plan.

## THE MASTER PLAN

A master plan shows the hard scape areas and planting beds, just as you want them to look.

Tape a clean sheet of tracing paper over your concept plan, and choose one of the bubbled areas. Sketch the hard scape elements first. This is the time to decide whether you want to entertain on a deck or patio. In the example above, the natural surroundings and fall of the terrain at the rear of the house would make a deck easier to build than a patio—the deck can be supported on posts, requiring little or no grading. While you're at it, play with different designs until you get a configuration that is both attractive and functional.

The addition of the deck in the example means that the play area will have to move from the lower level of the yard to an area close by, corresponding to a family-fun area.

Don't dwell on any zone too long. Just get the basic ingredients down, then draw the details.

After you've sketched the hard scape, it's time to draw planting beds. Wrap them around the hard scape and connect them with your pathway. Start by drawing the general contours of the path, then when you've finalized them, draw the pattern of materials. Be sure to maintain convenient indoor/outdoor access to the new additions in your design. Even if you complete only one aspect of the plan at a time, you can be assured that everything will eventually work together in harmony.

*Constructing a path is hard work. Excavating soil for a 5×25-foot path can mean moving up to 3 cubic yards of dirt. Enlist help on large projects and use your dimensioned plan as a guide.*

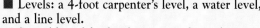

## BASIC TOOLS YOU'LL NEED

If you have any experience with yard maintenance, you probably own some or most of the items listed below. If you need to buy tools, get the best you can afford. Cheap tools wear out quickly and are more likely to break, which can make them dangerous. Rent tools you might not need in the future, and be sure to ask the rental staff how to use a tool you're not familiar with. The tools required for building your path will vary a little depending on the materials. You'll need:

■ Levels: a 4-foot carpenter's level, a water level, and a line level.
■ Screed board for leveling materials. Make your own, using the information shown on page 55.
■ Sturdy garden rake for moving gravel, sand, and loose materials.
■ Trowels: Depending on your path, you may need both digging and concrete-finishing trowels. Add a mortar bag to the list if installing brick, tile, or stone.
■ Wheelbarrow: a must for moving soil and materials, and you can mix small quantities of concrete in it.
■ Tamper to compact bedding. Build your own for small projects or rent a power tamper (see page 55).
■ Cans of marking spray paint that paint on the ground when held upside down.
■ Garden hose to help you lay out curved paths.
■ Tape measure: If you don't own a quality tape, buy one with a 1-inch-wide blade. You will use it a lot.
■ Pin flags for marking layouts.
■ Batter boards or wood stakes for laying out straight paths and squaring corners.
■ Shovels: a round-nosed shovel for excavating and spreading material, a square shovel or spade for leveling rough spots and removing sod.
■ Pick or mattock for loosening soil and rock.
■ Mason's line to mark straight paths.
■ Plumb bob to help mark corners.

# CONSTRUCTION BASICS

Once you've finished the plans, you're ready to tackle the actual installation of the path. Some steps are basic to all paths and materials. Each pathway, with the exception of a grass path, will require layout, excavation, pouring and leveling base materials, and placing the surface layer. Some paths will also require forms and edgings.

This chapter shows all the steps common to all forms of path building. Steps that pertain to specific materials are covered in the next chapter.

Before you start construction, schedule your material delivery. Arrange the delivery date so you have plenty of time to complete the preparation. That way you can have the materials delivered close to the work site, eliminating the need to store them on the driveway or patio and to move them to the project area yourself.

If you do need to store materials, keep them safe. Store bags of concrete mix where they won't get wet. Fence off piled flagstone or lumber with yellow construction tape so children and visitors won't stumble into it. Keep brick and stone on the pallets and don't cut the steel bands until you're ready to lay the material. To young children, a pallet of brick or stone can look like an inviting place to play.

Consider the size of the project and recruit a crew of helpers, if possible. This is especially important when pouring ready-mix concrete. Although you can take your time with concrete you mix yourself, you can't with ready-mix. Once the truck arrives, you have to get the concrete into the forms quickly.

## SAFETY FIRST

No matter what kind of path you choose, you'll be using tools that are made to cut and pound. Make sure you follow these basic safety precautions.
■ Wear heavy work boots with over-the-ankle support to protect your feet from dropped materials and twisting missteps. Steel-toe boots are worth the extra expense.
■ Durable, flexible gloves and denim clothing will protect your skin. Better yet, wear work clothes with pockets to keep small tools handy.
■ Wear goggles when sawing, hammering, or using power tools. A respirator or dust mask will keep airborne particles out of your lungs.
■ Plug electrical power tools into ground fault circuit interrupter (GFCI) outlets. They cut power immediately if they detect a short or human contact.
■ Keep a first-aid kit handy.
■ Wear a tool belt and keep your tools in it to save time and frustration.
■ Keep blades and edges sharp on all cutting tools, including shovels. Dull edges overwork the tool and the worker. Bring a file along to the work site and periodically sharpen the edges of shovels and spades.
■ Check before you dig. Find out where the utility lines are before you start putting in your path. Most utility companies will locate the lines for you at no charge.

# LAYOUT AND EXCAVATION

Laying out your path along its actual location is a matter of transferring its contour from your scaled drawing to the ground. Doing that requires careful work. You may not be able to make marks on soil as precisely as you can on paper, but the more attention you pay to your layout, the easier the remaining steps will be.

Plotting the corners and edges is the first step, whether you're building a straight or a curved path.

## PLOTTING A STRAIGHT PATH

Refer to the illustration below as you follow these steps:

■ Drive preliminary stakes into the ground at points that represent the approximate corners of the path. Use the width of the path—including the width of any forms or edging—to determine their locations.

■ Make batter boards by fastening an 18-inch 2×4 crosspiece to two 28-inch 2×4s pointed at the bottom. Drive the batter boards into the soil on each side of the temporary stakes and about 18 inches behind them. Make sure the

boards are firmly in the ground. Tie a mason's line taut between the batter boards. Level the batter boards using a line level or, on paths longer than 10 feet, a water level.

■ Square the corners with a 3-4-5 triangle. At each intersection, measure out 3 feet on

## PLOTTING A STRAIGHT PATH

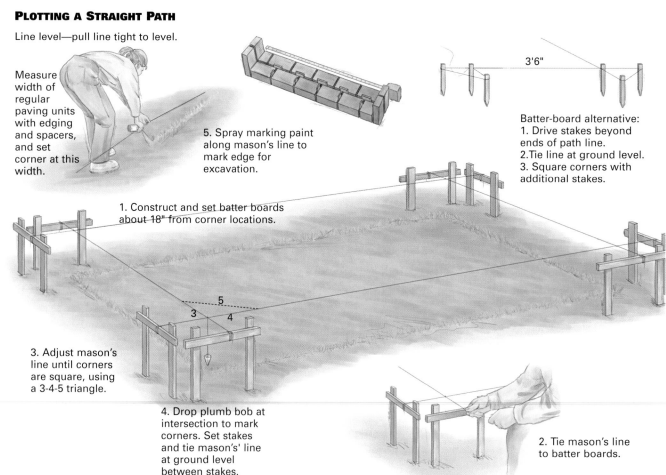

Line level—pull line tight to level.

Measure width of regular paving units with edging and spacers, and set corner at this width.

5. Spray marking paint along mason's line to mark edge for excavation.

3'6"

Batter-board alternative:
1. Drive stakes beyond ends of path line.
2. Tie line at ground level.
3. Square corners with additional stakes.

1. Construct and set batter boards about 18" from corner locations.

3. Adjust mason's line until corners are square, using a 3-4-5 triangle.

4. Drop plumb bob at intersection to mark corners. Set stakes and tie mason's' line at ground level between stakes.

2. Tie mason's line to batter boards.

## PLOTTING A CURVED PATH

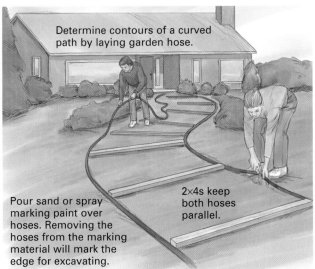

Determine contours of a curved path by laying garden hose.

Pour sand or spray marking paint over hoses. Removing the hoses from the marking material will mark the edge for excavating.

2x4s keep both hoses parallel.

## EXCAVATING FOR A PATH

Remove sod in strips with square shovel or spade. Replant sod in other areas of lawn.

Remove soil with round-nosed shovel.

Painted layout line

Batter boards

Till or loosen compacted soil with a pick. Drive pick into unexcavated soil and pull it toward you into excavated area.

one line and 4 feet on the other, using tape to mark the measurements on the lines. Now measure diagonally between the marks. If the distance is 5 feet, the corner is square. If it's not, loosen the mason's line and slide it on the crosspiece until the distance between the two marks is exactly 5 feet.

■ At each intersection, drop a plumb bob and move the preliminary stake to the point at which the plumb bob comes to rest. Tie another line between the stakes at ground level. This line represents the exact outline of your path. Remove the batter boards and upper mason's lines.

■ Using spray marking paint (available at your hardware store), mark the ground. If the surface of the path will be sloped, raise the mason's line to the proper angle and use it as a guide to set forms or edging. (See page 58 for more information about slopes.)

## PLOTTING A CURVED PATH

To plot the contours of a curved path:
■ Outline the edges with garden hose, spacers, and paint, as shown in the illustration above. Make sure the outline includes the width of edging or forms.
■ You can make precise arcs with a homemade landscape compass.

To make a compass, drive a stake in the ground at the point that represents the center of the circle of the arc, and tie a rope to it. Use your scaled plan to locate this point. Tie another sharp stake to the other end of the rope at a point that represents the edge of the path and scribe the grass with it. Keep the stake in the ground and retie the pointer farther out on the rope by the width of your path, then scribe another line.
■ No matter which method you use, mark the path contour with paint.

## BREAKING GROUND

Excavating the soil requires more than brute strength. There is some science to it.
■ Using a square shovel or spade, cut the sod along the painted outline of your path. Divide the width into 1-foot strips. Dig down 2 inches to preserve the roots. Slide the shovel under the sod to cut the roots away, and roll up the sod strips. Store the sod in the shade and replant it in other areas.
■ Use a rototiller set to the depth of the path materials to loosen the soil. Then, using a round-edged shovel and working across the entire width between the painted edges, dig out the soil to the depth equal to the combined thickness of all the materials. (See individual path instructions for correct depth.) Use a pick to loosen compacted or rocky soil. If the soil is suitable for planting, spread it on the bed. Tamp the soil remaining in the excavation to provide a firm surface for the gravel base.

## EDGING— NOW OR LATER?

Most materials will require you to set the edging first, before the surface. Concrete is the main exception. Install the edging on a concrete path after the slab cures completely.

Edging materials such as flagstone, landscape timbers, and other hard materials should be set on the gravel base to allow proper drainage. With this installation, digging separate side trenches for the edging is not necessary.

Fill the excavation with the gravel base material to a height that will put the top of the edging slightly below ground level, set the edging, and add more base material if needed (see page 56).

# LAYING THE SUBBASE

Subbase materials, typically gravel and sand, serve several purposes in any path installation.

The gravel base, usually from 4 to 6 inches thick, provides a solid foundation for the materials. It also lets water drain away from the surface, reducing rot and moss formation and increasing safety. And while you're building the path, the gravel keeps the excavation from becoming a mud pit in the rain.

The sand layer, about 2 inches thick, also acts as a drainage medium, provides a smooth surface for laying paving materials, and allows uneven paving like flagstone to be set with its surface level and flat.

In between these two layers lies landscape fabric, a permeable material that keeps the sand from migrating into the gravel and helps deter weed growth in the path. Landscape fabrics are available in several widths from your local landscape retail outlet. Purchase a size slightly wider than your path. You can cut it to fit with scissors.

## LAYING THE GRAVEL BASE

Once you have excavated the soil for the path—you will find the specific depths for each type of path in the next chapter—cut away roots and remove protruding rocks.

Bring gravel to the excavation with a wheelbarrow and pour or shovel it in. Gravel can be surprisingly stubborn when you try to move it around. A round-nosed shovel works best. Do your final leveling with a garden rake.

If you've determined that your soil drains poorly (see page 16), use washed gravel for the base. If drainage is not a problem, use crusher-run gravel. It's used in road construction, costs less, and packs into a solid base. It won't allow much water to pass through, however, so don't let its low cost be the sole determining factor when choosing a base material.

Fill the excavation to a depth that will put the top of the edging material at or slightly above ground level (or higher if your design calls for it). Make the surface as level as you can with the shovel, step it down by walking on it, and tamp it with a homemade or power tamper (see "Using a Power Tamper" on the opposite page). If your path is set on a slope, work from the bottom to the top, compacting loose material against that already firmed up.

Set in a few trial pieces of edging and add more gravel if necessary to build it to the desired height. Set forms now if your design calls for them. When the base is thick enough to raise the edging to the correct height, install all the edging. For more information on how to put in different edgings and forms, see page 56. Add more gravel between the edging if necessary to bring the paving material to the correct height.

## THE WEED BARRIER

Weeds can grow almost anywhere, and although you may not be able to thwart their pesky presence entirely, you can slow them down significantly with a layer of landscape fabric. Use any of several varieties of nonwoven barrier material—it's tough and won't break down as easily as woven fabric. Cut the fabric so it extends fully between the pieces of edging material. Overlap seams by at least a foot.

**SPREADING AND TAMPING GRAVEL**

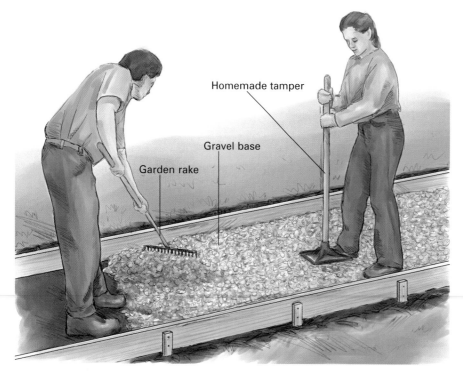

Homemade tamper

Gravel base

Garden rake

**LAYING THE SAND BASE**

Garden rake

Sand

Gravel

**SCREEDING THE SAND BASE**

Beveled stakes allow screed to pass.

2×4 or 2×6 with edges notched to slide over forms

## ADDING THE SAND

Bring sand to the site and pour or shovel it into the excavation with a round-nosed shovel. Use a garden rake to level it about an inch thick. Dampen, but do not soak, the sand with a hose and fine-spray nozzle. Then tamp the sand. Repeat, adding sand, dampening, and tamping, until the layer is about 2 inches thick.

Do your final leveling with a screed. Make the screed from a 2×4 or 2×6 that's long enough to span the width of the path. Cut out notches at each end (shown in the photo at right). The notches

should be wide enough to allow you to move the screed from side to side as you level. Make the notches deep enough so the bottom of the screed will level the sand at the height required for your materials—generally even with or slightly below the top of the edging.

Screeding will go smoothly if you have installed wooden forms. It is more difficult with rough edging. For edging with extremely rough surfaces, use a board that fits inside the edging. In any case, screeding always works better with two people—one on each end.

### FLAG THE SITE

Don't take chances with an open excavation. Mark your work site clearly so visitors or children do not injure themselves by falling into it. At the end of each workday, drive four stakes around the perimeter and tie yellow construction tape to them.

### USING A POWER TAMPER

A homemade tamper works fine in small installations, but for larger paths and more complete compacting of materials, you should rent a power tamper.

Ask the rental outlet staff to show you how to start and operate it. They might help you load it into your vehicle (better bring a pickup), but you'll need help unloading it when you get home.

Be careful when using a power tamper. You're not likely to lose control of the machine, but it can seriously injure your feet. Do not use it without wearing steel-toe boots.

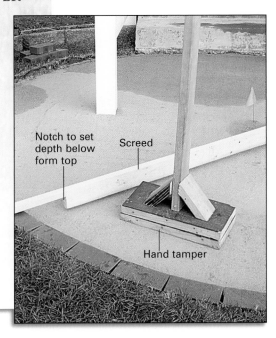

Notch to set depth below form top

Screed

Hand tamper

# EDGING AND FORMS

Edging helps define the contours of your path and is often part of the overall design. When choosing the materials for edging, don't limit yourself to the same material used for the paving. Brick contrasts nicely with loose stone and natural paths. So does landscape timber. And even a concrete curb can be decorative if you color it and set aggregates in it before it's cured.

Edging, of course, also adds a practical element to path construction, keeping materials—especially mulches and loose stone—from creeping into the surrounding lawn or flower beds.

Forms are primarily practical. You'll need a form for any installation involving concrete, whether the slab will function as the finished surface of the path or act as the base for mortared brick or stone.

## SHAPING THE CURVES

Curved forms are easy to make. You can use one of three products:
- Benderboard—a thin wood composite that comes in various thicknesses and is available at your home center. Use material at least 3/8 inch thick when forming concrete. Two layers are sturdier than one.
- Homemade benderboard—1× stock with saw kerfs crosscut about every 1/2 inch and about 1/2 inch deep. The saw kerfs allow you to bend the stock around the stakes you've set in the excavation.
- Flexible material—preformed plastic or steel, some types of which are made with feet or lugs through which you drive spikes to anchor it.

In other installations, forms are optional. For example, you can set brick soldiers (installed vertically) and sailors (laid flat) without forms if your excavation line is precise. Some soils, especially loose or rocky varieties, won't support edging. In these soils, set forms so that your bricks or other materials don't wander off the mark.

## TIPS FOR EDGES AND FORMS

- Always include the width of the edging or form when laying out and marking your excavation. Dig out the soil to the complete width of the path, including the edging.
- Dig out at an angle about a foot of soil beyond the path edge to allow room to fasten the form boards to the stakes.

## STAKING STRAIGHT FORMS

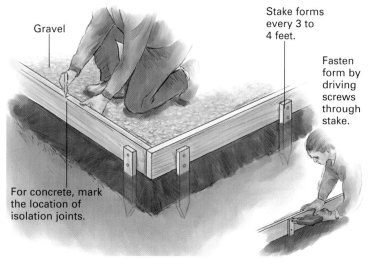

Gravel

Stake forms every 3 to 4 feet.

Fasten form by driving screws through stake.

For concrete, mark the location of isolation joints.

## STAKING CURVED FORMS

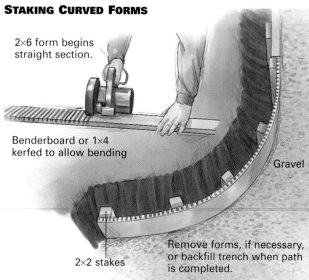

2×6 form begins straight section.

Benderboard or 1×4 kerfed to allow bending

Gravel

2×2 stakes

Remove forms, if necessary, or backfill trench when path is completed.

**INSTALLING PREFORMED EDGING**

1. Excavate and lay gravel base.

2. Set stakes as guides for contours. Install edging. Remove stakes.

5. Backfill trench.

4. Lay paving material.

3. Lay sand bed and tamp.

## INSTALLING BRICK EDGING

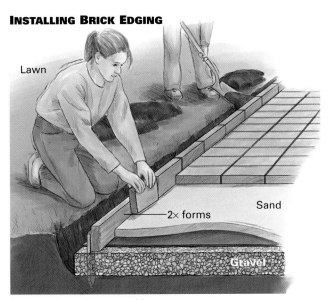

Lawn

2× forms

Sand

Gravel

1. Excavate and lay gravel base.
2. Drive stakes every 3 to 4 feet and attach 2× forms.
3. Lay sand base and tamp.
4. Set brick edging.
5. Set one or two rows of paving as you go.
6. Remove forms and backfill.

## INSTALLING TIMBER EDGING

1. Excavate to depth required for paving and gravel.
2. Predrill timbers for ½" rebar.
3. Set timbers at edge of excavation.
4. Drive in rebar.
5. Set pavement.

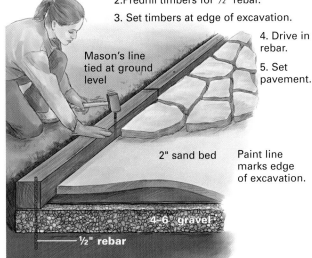

Mason's line tied at ground level

2" sand bed

Paint line marks edge of excavation.

4–6" gravel

½" rebar

■ If possible, leave the ground-level marking line in place until the form is set.

■ Set edging materials on the gravel base, not on trenches dug at the side of the excavation. This will allow water to drain away from the edging, as well as the paving material.

■ Always set stakes on the outer surface of the forms and drive galvanized screws through the stake and into the form board. Nailing the form to the stakes could dislodge them.

■ Where possible, set forms below the ground surface and cover them with topsoil when the path is completed. For example, 2×4 forms set below the surface will provide enough support for brick soldiers. You can leave the forms in place and cover them. Always use treated lumber rated for ground contact if you will leave the lumber in the ground.

■ Whether covering the forms or removing them, use topsoil to backfill behind the form.

■ Set edging material no more than ½ inch above ground level to allow easier mowing.

■ When sloping a path to improve drainage, install one form slightly lower than the other.

## INSTALLING A CONCRETE CURB

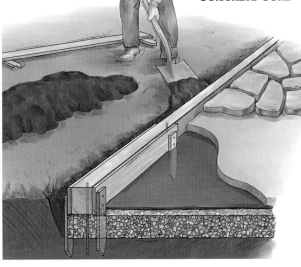

1. Excavate to depth of concrete and gravel.
2. Lay gravel subbase.
3. Drive stakes.
4. Attach forms to stakes.
5. Pour concrete and finish edge.
6. Remove forms.
7. Backfill trench.
8. Lay paving.

## INSTALLING FLAGSTONE EDGING

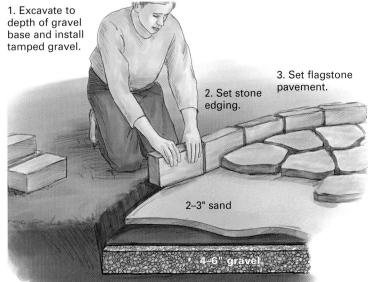

1. Excavate to depth of gravel base and install tamped gravel.
2. Set stone edging.
3. Set flagstone pavement.

2–3" sand

4–6" gravel

# SLOPES AND DRAINAGE

## FINDING THE SLOPE

1. Drive stakes firmly into ground at top and bottom of slope.

2. Tie mason's line to top stake at ground level.

3. Tie the other end of the mason's line to the bottom stake. Use a line level to keep it level.

4. At the bottom stake, measure the distance from the line to the ground. Divide this measurement by the distance between the stakes. The result is the percentage of slope.

A 2 percent slope

¼"

12"

Line level

If you're building a path on a relatively flat area, you don't have to worry much about slopes or drainage. All you have to do is clear the site, perhaps smooth it a little, and crown the surface materials for drainage.

Few landscapes are perfectly flat, of course. If your path site slopes—or if you're doing major landscape redesigning—planning and construction are a little more complicated.

### CALCULATING THE SLOPE

When you're planning your path and laying it out, pay careful attention to the slope of the land. If your path site slopes gently, set a course that will allow natural water runoff. Ideally, the path surface should slope both across its width and along its length by 3 or 4 percent—a slope of about 1 inch every 3 or 4 feet. This slope will be almost imperceptible to the eye and easy to walk on, and it will allow proper drainage.

Here's how to determine how much your land slopes. Drive stakes at the top and bottom of the slope and tie a level mason's line tightly between them as shown in the illustration above.

At the bottom stake, measure the distance from the line to the ground. Divide this measurement by the distance between the stakes (in the same unit of measurement) then multiply by 100 to calculate the percentage of slope. For example, if the terrain drops 6 inches over a distance of 20 feet (240 inches), that's a 2.5 percent slope. Compare your calculation with the following guidelines to get an idea of what corrective action, if any, you need to take.

■ Less than 1.5 percent—will probably need cross-path drainage.
■ 1.5 to 5 percent—an excellent site for a path.
■ 5 to 8 percent—steep enough to require steps.
■ More than 8 percent—too steep for a path without steps or landings.

### TAMING SLOPES

Siting a path on most slopes won't be as difficult as it might first seem to be. For example, weaving the path across a slope will not only make it easier to use, it will add to the visual interest. Refer to the

## TAMING A SLOPE

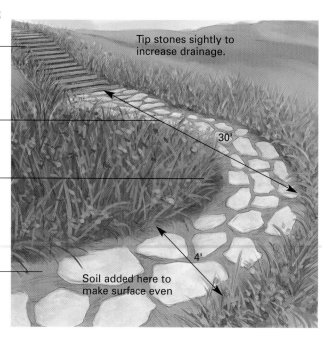

Slope is 10 percent—too steep without steps installed.

Slope drops 1 foot over distance of 30 feet from upper end to lower end, a 3 percent slope.

Contour of path curves around the base of a slight incline, avoids cutting into the bank, and keeps the pitch of the walk constant.

Path weaves across terrain to reduce incline.

Tip stones sightly to increase drainage.

30'

4'

Soil added here to make surface even

illustration at left for some common methods of siting a pathway on sloping ground. When a path runs perpendicular to extremely steep terrain, install retaining walls to keep the surface flat.

If you do have to cut into the slope to even out the course of the path, dig soil from elevated areas in the site to fill depressions whenever possible. When filling a depression, add soil a little at a time, tamping as you go.

## WHERE SHOULD THE WATER GO?

Poor drainage can ruin the best landscape designs, but you can correct most drainage problems with a few simple techniques.

**Swale:** A swale is a narrow, shallow ditch that diverts surface water around structures or other features. Building a swale is easy—simply remove the sod and 3–4 inches of soil (see illustration, right). You can finish a swale with concrete or make it less noticeable by replanting the sod or seeding grass in the bottom.

**French drain:** A french drain removes surface water from low or boggy areas and takes it to another location (see illustration, below right).

Excavate to a depth of at least 1 foot, but make sure that the pipe slopes at least ⅛ inch per foot to its terminal point.

Place 2 inches of coarse aggregate under the pipe and another 6 inches on top. Install the perforated pipe with the perforations down, and put landscape fabric over the pipe to keep soil from clogging it. Finish the drain with exposed gravel or by covering it with 2 to 3 inches of topsoil, then sod or seed.

Let the pipe *daylight* (open to the surface) at lower ground—but not on the neighbor's property—or run it into a dry well.

**Dry well:** A dry well is an underground water-collection device (see the illustration on the next page). A dry well is essentially a large hole filled with coarse aggregate. Local codes will specify different sizes, based on average rainfall data. The specifications shown in the illustration will comply with most codes, but you should check with your local building department before digging. Dry wells are especially useful where you can't legally or conveniently let an underground drain line discharge on the surface.

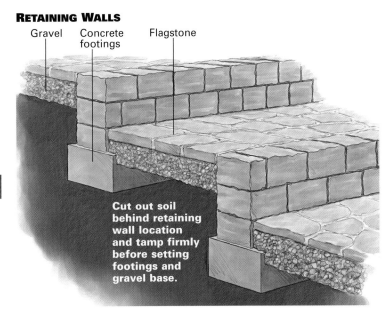

### RETAINING WALLS
Gravel  Concrete footings  Flagstone

Cut out soil behind retaining wall location and tamp firmly before setting footings and gravel base.

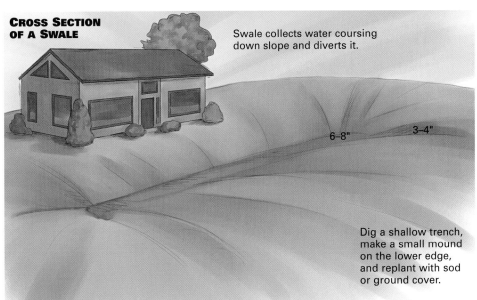

### CROSS SECTION OF A SWALE
Swale collects water coursing down slope and diverts it.

6–8"  3–4"

Dig a shallow trench, make a small mound on the lower edge, and replant with sod or ground cover.

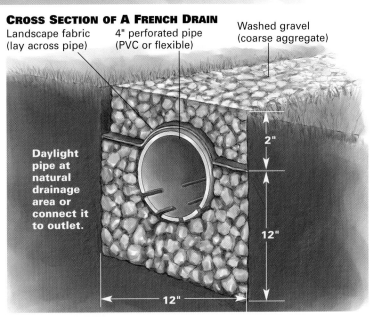

### CROSS SECTION OF A FRENCH DRAIN
Landscape fabric (lay across pipe)  4" perforated pipe (PVC or flexible)  Washed gravel (coarse aggregate)

Daylight pipe at natural drainage area or connect it to outlet.

2"  12"  12"

# SLOPES AND DRAINAGE
*continued*

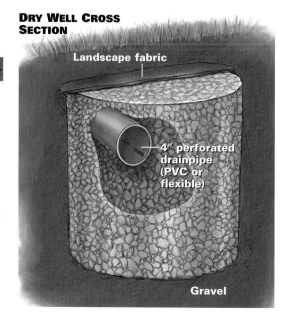

## DRAINING THE PATH

Even on flat ground, paths need to let water run off. The easiest way to speed surface drainage is to crown the paving slightly (see illustration, opposite page). Build up the sand or supporting layer toward the center of the path to crown the materials.

On paths that traverse slopes, place the downhill edge lower than the uphill edge. This is easier when using forms to support the edging, giving you a hard surface to lay your level on so you can see how much the path slopes to the lower side.

To maintain the slope down the hill, make a gauge from a 2×4 cut to the width of your path. Taper the board from end to end at the angle of the slope. Set the board on the path with a level on top. When the bubble is centered, the slope is correct.

Whether you should add a drainage system to your path depends on how well your soil drains. See page 16 for information on testing your soil. If your soil drains poorly, consider the easy-to-install drainage line illustrated at the top of the opposite page. It works for any bedding material.

On paths that slope steeply, build a trough from pressure-treated lumber rated for ground contact—2×6s fastened to the edges of a 2×8 base with galvanized screws or nails. Lay the trough perpendicular to the path and fill it with gravel. Water will run off to the lowest side. Such a trough will also add an interesting accent to your path.

## MAKING A DRAIN-LINE SLOPE GAUGE

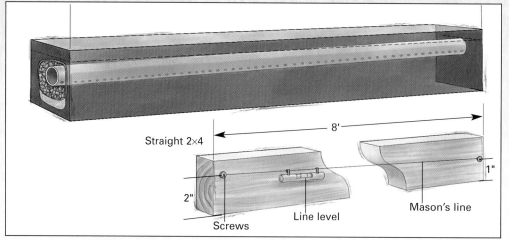

Any time you're installing a drain line, make sure it slopes correctly. This tool will make checking the slope easy.

Predrill holes for #8×1-inch screws about an inch from each end of a straight 8-foot 2×4. Position the holes from the top and bottom edges as shown above, and drive the screws almost completely into the board. Tie a

mason's line tightly between the screws and clip a line level to the line at the top end.

Check the slope of your drain line excavation by laying the tool in the trench. When the bubble is centered in the level, the board slopes 1 inch in 8 feet, or a little more than 1 percent. Add or remove gravel to adjust the line's slope.

## IN-PATH DRAINAGE

If you are constructing a path along the bottom of a steep incline, in a depression, or in any other area where severe runoff can cause the path to flood, lay a drain line in your base material.

Begin by excavating deep enough to accommodate the drain line and still provide adequate support for the materials above. Sloping the bottom of the trench slightly toward the center will cause the water to run more quickly into the pipe.

Lay in about 2 inches of gravel and tamp it. Any washed gravel will do, but do not use crusher-run stone, which compacts into a hard layer and won't drain well. Then lay the perforated drain pipe in the center of the site with the perforations down. The perforations go on the bottom to allow water to drain quickly as it fills the trench.

Now spread more gravel, adding about 2 inches at a time and tamping as you go. Make sure you have at least 2 inches of gravel above the pipe. Stop when you've reached a depth that will leave the paving materials at the correct height.

Cut a piece of landscape fabric wide enough to span the site and lay it on the gravel. The fabric will help keep weeds down and stop the sand from

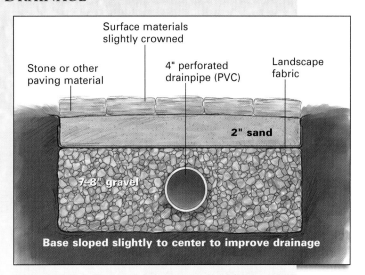

Surface materials slightly crowned

Stone or other paving material

4" perforated drainpipe (PVC)

Landscape fabric

2" sand

7–8" gravel

**Base sloped slightly to center to improve drainage**

migrating into the gravel base. Plug the top end to keep soil from washing into the pipe, and screen the bottom end to keep small animals from entering.

Complete the installation with sand and the paving material.

## UNDERGROUND UTILITIES

If outdoor lighting or other improvements—such as irrigation lines or power lines for a pool or work shed—are part of your plans for the future, install utility runways under the path when you build it.

Creating the runways won't take more than about 15 minutes and will save you the time, trouble, and effort of digging up the path later or finding an alternate, more expensive route.

Use a piece of 2- to 4-inch PVC pipe cut about 12 to 16 inches longer than the width of your path. Get the larger size now if you're not sure about your future needs.

Cover the ends of the pipe with heavy tape (duct tape works fine) to keep dirt and base materials out of the pipe. Wrap the ends of the tape with stove wire or other flexible wire to keep it in place after the adhesive eventually loses strength.

Shovel about 2 inches of gravel into the excavation and tamp it. Then, using your plans as a guide, position the runway in the gravel bed at an angle convenient for the future utilities. If necessary, dig a recess at the edge of your path to allow the pipe to fit. Continue adding gravel and finish materials. Drive a large framing nail at both edges of the path so you can find the runway when you need it.

When you install the utility line, dig its trench to the ends of the runway, remove the wire and tape, then push the line through.

Concrete slab or other path material

Large framing nails mark the location of the runway for future use.

6–8"

6–8"

2–4" PVC pipe for wiring

Gravel base

Wire

# STEPPING UP TO THE PATH

Steps make slopes easier to climb and add a dramatic accent to the path. Design your steps as an integral part of the path, and pick materials that complement its style.

Building landscape steps is different from building indoor stairs. Indoor stairs allow no leeway in their calculations, but landscape steps can be adjusted to fit.

Landscape steps should be gradual—short risers with deep treads are preferred. (*Tread* refers to the horizontal part of the step where you place your feet. Vertical *risers* separate one tread from the other.) To climb steep slopes—10 percent or more—construct a series of steps with landings at least 30 inches deep. If you slope each landing a little, the climb will feel gentle, and you may be able to reduce the overall number of steps. Let each tread overhang the riser below by about 1 inch. This overhang is the architectural detail that shows that a step is ahead.

**THE RISE AND RUN OF A SLOPE**

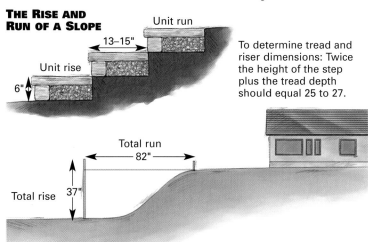

Unit run

13–15"

Unit rise

6"

To determine tread and riser dimensions: Twice the height of the step plus the tread depth should equal 25 to 27.

Total run
82"

Total rise   37"

## RISE AND RUN

The first thing to do when planning steps is to figure the rise and run—the dimensions for the tread and risers.

Here's how to compute them:

■ Drive stakes at the top and bottom of the slope, and measure the horizontal distance between them, as shown at left. This is the total *run* of the steps.

■ Tie a mason's line to the top stake at ground level and to the bottom stake, keeping the line level across the span. Measure the distance from the ground to the line on the bottom stake. This is the total *rise*.

■ Calculate the unit rise. Divide the total rise by 6 inches—the standard, comfortable height for outdoor steps. Round the result up to the nearest whole number. This is the number of 6-inch risers needed for the slope.

In the example, divide the total 37-inch rise by 6, which results in 6.1 risers. Round that up to 7.

Now divide the rise again by the number of steps (7), which in this example results in a riser height of approximately 5¼ inches—a little lower than the ideal 6 inches. (It's better to be a little lower than too high.)

## TRIP-PROOF STEPS

Outdoor steps will be comfortable to climb if twice the riser height plus the tread depth is from 25 to 27 inches. That works out to a tread depth of 13 to 15 inches for a standard 6-inch rise. (2×6=12; 12+13=25; 12+15=27.) After you complete your preliminary calculations, adjust the rise and run of your stairs to get to 25 to 27 inches, and you're sure to have safe and comfortable landscape stairs.

## SELECTING STONES

If you are building flagstone steps, use stones from 2 to 4 inches thick, smooth-surfaced and coarse-textured. Such stones make ample, safe walking surfaces. If the front edges protrude, cut them so they are even with the front surface. If you can't find stones that are equally thick, you can make up the difference with different-sized risers. A 3-inch step over a 3-inch riser results in the same overall height as a 2-inch step over 4-inch risers.

Flagstone steps are heavy. To make your stair-building efforts less strenuous, have these large stones delivered at the top of the site, not the bottom.

You will begin installing them at the bottom, of course, but sliding them down the slope will be much easier than hauling them to the top.

Avoid tearing up the surrounding turf by laying an 8-foot sheet of plywood next to the site and pushing or pulling the stone steps into place.

■ Calculate the unit run next. To figure the unit run, divide the total run by the number of steps from the first calculation.

In the example, divide the total 82-inch run by 7, resulting in tread of about 11¾ inches. You can adjust both figures slightly to assure a comfortable climb (see "Trip-Proof Steps" on the opposite page).

In the example, you could safely install 6-inch risers and 13-inch treads or 5-inch risers with 15-inch treads, making small adjustments in the path to keep the steps equal and at the correct height.

## BUILDING THE STEPS

Building steps in your landscape will require the same general methods used in construction of the path—layout, excavation, and installation of the base materials.

All step materials require a stable gravel base for support and drainage. Mortared steps need a concrete base, so you'll have to build forms. The illustration at right will give you a general idea of how to build your steps.

### TYPICAL STEP CONSTRUCTION

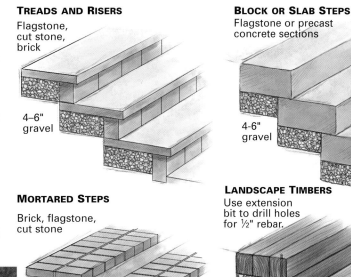

**TREADS AND RISERS**
Flagstone, cut stone, brick
4–6" gravel

**BLOCK OR SLAB STEPS**
Flagstone or precast concrete sections
4-6" gravel

**MORTARED STEPS**
Brick, flagstone, cut stone
1–2" mortar bed
Cast concrete base

**LANDSCAPE TIMBERS**
Use extension bit to drill holes for ½" rebar.
½-inch rebar
4-6" gravel

Tread surface can be any material. Loose material should be set below rear surface of tread and edged on the sides.

For more detailed instructions, see the specific sections in the next chapter.

## LAYING OUT STEPS

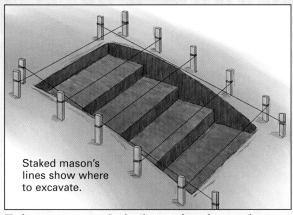

Staked mason's lines show where to excavate.

To lay out steps in the landscape, first drive stakes at both sides of the path, spacing them at a distance equal to the depth of the tread and the width of the path, including edging. Tie mason's line tightly between the stakes, both across and down the path.

Remove the sod from each level and, starting at the bottom, dig down to a depth equal to the thickness of your base and paving materials. Use the mason's lines and a level as guides to make sure the soil in each section is level.

## MAKING CONCRETE PADS

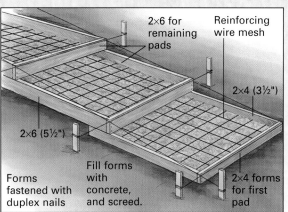

2×6 for remaining pads
Reinforcing wire mesh
2×4 (3½")
2×6 (5½")
Forms fastened with duplex nails
Fill forms with concrete, and screed.
2×4 forms for first pad

Concrete pads make an easy base for mortared steps. Excavate the area as shown in the illustration at left, allowing for the thickness of the forms. Using duplex nails, preassemble the forms for each pad. Note that the first pad is constructed from 2×4s and the remaining pads are 2×6s. As shown, these pads will accommodate 2-inch bricks and result in a 6-inch riser. Rip 2× stock to accommodate different material thicknesses. Fasten the forms to stakes with screws, install rebar and wire mesh, pour concrete, and screed.

# CONCRETE BASICS

Concrete, a mixture of sand, gravel, portland cement, and water, is the most versatile material you can use to build a path. You can form it into almost any contour or shape and use it either as the base for mortared materials or the finished surface itself. Modern finishing techniques can make concrete surfaces look remarkably like flagstone, brick, old stone pavers, and other hard materials. Its chief drawback is that mistakes are not easy to correct.

## PLANNING THE JOB

Unless you mix it yourself, concrete is the one material you shouldn't lay in stages. Even when you mix your own, it's better to pour all the concrete the same day—when all the materials, tools, and helpers are on-site and arranged. So if you're planning concrete or mortared walks both in front and in back of the house, make sure both sites are ready at the same time—excavations completed, forms made, and reinforcements in place.

Should you mix your own or call for a ready-mix truck? Generally it's cost effective to mix your own if your project doesn't need more than a ¼ yard of concrete. You can do this easily using premixed bags or combining the dry-mix ingredients yourself in a wheelbarrow or power mixer.

You should order ready-mix for projects of a yard or more. For those amounts in between, you may also want to have the material delivered. To mix ⅔ yard of concrete, enough to cover an 18×4-foot walk, you'll have to shovel and mix about 370 pounds of cement, 900 pounds of sand, 1,300 pounds of gravel, and 180 pounds of water.

## BUILDING THE FORMS

If you're pouring a slab for a mortared path, you may be tempted to skip building forms and pour directly into the excavation. You'll get more precise results with forms, however. If the concrete will serve as the finished surface, you must use forms.

Refer to the illustrations on the opposite page and on page 56. Keep these tips in mind when building concrete forms:

■ Align the inside edges of the forms with the layout lines.

■ Brace all forms securely: Set diagonal kickers every 6 feet to keep the weight of the material from bowing the forms.

■ Drive stakes into the ground at least a foot deep so the forms won't float on the concrete.

■ Fasten the forms to the stakes, keeping the forms level throughout. Use a 4-foot level and tap down any errant boards.

■ Keep the top of the stakes below the form or saw the stakes off flush so you will have a smooth surface to pull the screed along.

■ When creating slopes, measure the slope carefully. Drive the lower form deeper into the ground by the amount of the slope.

■ Lubricate the inside faces of the forms with oil (used oil is fine) for easier removal.

■ Set fiber or mechanical expansion strips every 10 feet.

If your forms will remain as edging:

■ Use naturally resistant species or pressure-treated wood rated for ground contact (see page 38).

■ Before pouring the concrete, tape the exposed edge of permanent wood edging to keep the liquid concrete from staining it.

■ Drive 16d galvanized nails through the edging into the concrete to keep the edges of the form locked against the sides of the slab.

Once you have set the forms, shovel in a washed-gravel base, level it, and tamp it to a depth of 4 inches.

## WHAT'S IN A YARD?

Concrete is sold by the cubic yard, which is often just called a yard. A cubic yard is 3 feet long, wide, and deep, so it contains 27 cubic feet. A slab path 10 feet long, 4 feet wide, and 3 inches thick (.25 ft.) has a volume of a little over ⅓ cubic yard ($10 \times 4 \times .25 = 10/27 = .37$).

## A DRY-MIX RECIPE

If you're mixing your own batch from scratch, use this handy recipe:

    1 part portland cement
    2 parts sand
    3 parts gravel
    ½ part water

Mix all the dry ingredients together in a wheelbarrow or power mixer, then add water a little at a time. Concrete should have the consistency of a thick malt.

## CONCRETE ADDITIVES

Plain concrete will work just fine in moderate weather conditions. Extreme temperatures, however, both hot and cold, may make the mix unworkable and can cause it to cure improperly, crack, or even powder.

Engineers and chemists have developed additives that allow concrete to be poured in imperfect weather.

■ Air bubbles in the concrete (entrainment) help keep concrete from freezing when pouring in extreme cold.

■ Accelerators help concrete set up faster in cold weather.

■ Retardants slow down the curing when the weather gets hot.

■ Water reducers make the mix more workable, reducing time and labor on large jobs.

## BRINGING IN REINFORCEMENTS

Concrete has terrific compression strength, meaning it will withstand great, crushing forces. It has little tensile strength, however, and needs internal reinforcements to keep it from cracking. Once you have built the forms, bring in the reinforcements.

■ Set *dobies*—3-inch blocks used to keep reinforcing wire centered in the concrete—every 3 to 4 feet on the gravel base. You can use concrete paver pieces as dobies. Attach them to the mesh with tie wire. Dobies available from building supply dealers have a tie wire attached.

■ Lay down reinforcing mesh and tie it to the dobies. Use 10-gauge 6×6 mesh, which comes in rolls or flats, generally 5 feet wide. Rolled mesh costs less, but it's springy and can be very hard to work with. Precut flats of mesh are worth the slight extra expense.

Using a fencing pliers or heavy wire cutters, cut the mesh 4 inches shorter than the width of your path. Center the mesh between the forms, leaving 2 inches on each side.

## MAKING THE POUR

If you're mixing your own concrete, get two wheelbarrows—put one at the mixing site, use the other for pouring.

No matter how you bring the concrete to the site, these tips will make the job go more smoothly:

■ Dampen the gravel bed and forms to keep them from drawing moisture out of the mix.

■ Pour the farthest corners first, then work toward the truck or mixing area.

■ If you can't get a ready-mix truck within about 20 feet of the site, have the concrete pumped through a hose—it's worth the extra cost.

■ Fill depressions in the mix with shovelfuls, but don't throw the mix. Throwing can cause the aggregate to settle, weakening the surface.

■ Work shovels or 2×4s up and down in the concrete across the path to let the air out. Tap the forms on the side with a hammer about every 3 feet or so to help the concrete settle into any recesses.

■ Tamp the surface with a hoe to even it out. Don't overtamp or you'll bring too much water to the top.

**MIXING CONCRETE**

Water / Concrete mix / Mason's hoe

1. Add concrete to wheelbarrow, leaving a space at the rear.

2. Add water at the rear of the wheelbarrow.

3. Pull concrete mix into the water a little at a time. Mix thoroughly, pulling more concrete and adding more water as you go.

4. Finish by pulling liquid mix back and forth across wheelbarrow.

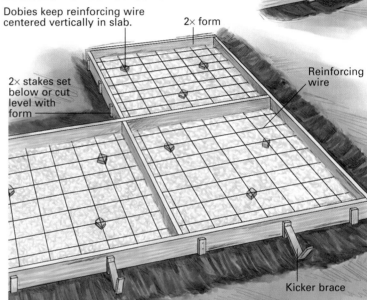

**BUILDING FORMS FOR CONCRETE**

Sheet metal or benderboard for tight curve (backfill to support)

Dobies keep reinforcing wire centered vertically in slab.

2× form

Reinforcing wire

2× stakes set below or cut level with form

Kicker brace

**POURING CONCRETE**

2×10 ramp

Start your pour at far corners of path.

Mason's hoe

Use a round-nosed shovel and mason's hoe to spread concrete evenly.

Tap form to settle concrete along perimeter.

# CONCRETE BASICS
*continued*

## SCREEDING THE CONCRETE

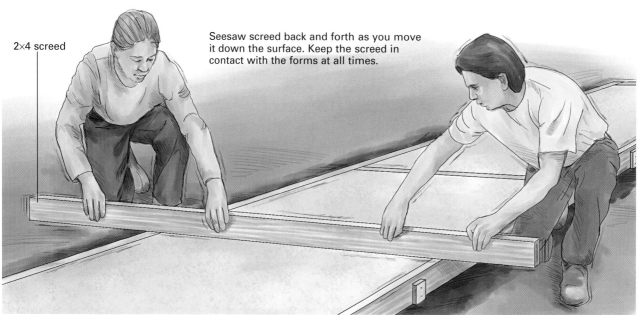

2×4 screed

Seesaw screed back and forth as you move it down the surface. Keep the screed in contact with the forms at all times.

## SCREEDING

Screeding or striking off the surface of the concrete levels it with the forms and provides a preliminary smoothing. It's a job best done by two people. Use a 2×4 about 1 foot longer than the width of the poured walk. Set the edge of the screed on the forms and draw the screed back and forth across the surface.

The first pass might leave humps or depressions. Fill in low spots and make a second pass, repeating the process until the surface is uniform.

## FLOATING THE SURFACE

Floating is the second smoothing, the one that pushes the aggregate below the surface. If you can reach the entire area from both sides, you can float it with a hand float or darby, as shown on the opposite page. Larger areas are easier to work with a bullfloat.

To use a float, push it away from you with the leading edge raised slightly off the surface. Pull the float back toward you, again with the leading edge raised. Move the float in arcs (but work a bullfloat back and forth). Overlap each pass until you have covered the area.

If you are going to lay tiles, pavers, or other materials in mortar on the slab, floating will leave the surface smooth enough. In fact, you should give it a slight tooth when it stiffens so

the mortar will adhere better. Push and pull a stiff-bristled driveway broom across the surface, applying slight pressure.

If the concrete will be a path surface, finish it as shown on pages 90–91.

## CUTTING EDGES

Wait for the water sheen to evaporate from the surface, and when it's gone, work a pointed trowel down about 1 inch between

## COLORING CONCRETE

Although you can color concrete by sprinkling stains or by painting the surface, surface colorants will eventually (sometimes quickly) wear off. Adding coloring agents to the mix before you pour it is more effective. Coloring agents tint the entire thickness of the slab and won't wear off. You can save a little money and effort by pouring uncolored concrete to within 2 inches of its final height, then pouring a 2-inch colored layer.

Pigments are made in a wide range of colors, and you can combine them to make tints to suit your taste. You'll find pigments at your building supply center in 5-, 25-, and 50-pound bags.

**FLOATING THE SURFACE**

Hand float

Darby

Bullfloat

the concrete and the forms. This will make the forms easier to pull away later.

Then run an edging tool back and forth along the inside of the forms. Edging rounds the concrete edge so it will resist cracking and chipping. Just as you did when floating, keep the tool's leading edge slightly raised.

## LAYING A MORTAR BASE

Brick, tile, flagstone, and cut stone will make a permanent, almost maintenance-free path if mortared to a concrete slab. Excavations for such installations, of course, will need to be deeper than for other paths. You're actually pouring a concrete walk—a pad below the materials to be mortared.

Pour the pad and let the concrete cure for three days to a week. Then, with a mason's trowel and a flat trowel, spread on a layer of mortar—about ½ inch for brick and tile, 1 inch for flagstone. Set the paving materials in the mortar with a slight twist and level them. Let the mortar cure overnight, and grout the joints with a mortar bag. See page 77 for more information on mortared paths.

## MAKING CONTROL JOINTS

Control joints are grooves in the concrete designed to control where it cracks. By cutting the surface of the concrete slightly with a jointing tool, you give the slab a place to crack underneath, without marring the surface. In general you should space control joints about 8 to 10 feet apart in a pathway slab.

## CURING

Concrete will harden rather rapidly. It will support your weight within a few hours. It does not reach full strength, however, for three to five days, depending on weather conditions.

The key to curing concrete is to keep moisture in it during the process. Either spray the surface lightly at periodic intervals or cover it with plastic, burlap, or roofing felt. Whatever material you use, tape or weight the covering against the sides of the slabs.

In extremely cold temperatures, you must keep the concrete from freezing for at least two days after you've poured it. Cover the surface with straw or blankets. Concrete gives off low-level heat when curing, and the straw or blankets will help hold the heat in and prevent the concrete from freezing.

You can wait until the slab is completely cured before removing the forms, but they will come off more easily after about two days.

*The most idyllic garden path almost always begins as a featureless area in a yard. A little imagination, a well-thought plan, and some work—starting with excavation and building forms—will bring beautiful results. Whether your path will be loose, natural material like this one, stone, brick, wood, or concrete, this chapter shows you how to build it.*

# BUILDING PATHS AND WALKWAYS

A professional builder always has a mental picture of the tasks a project requires. This is a learned skill, and anyone can take advantage of it with thorough planning. Anything you can do ahead of time to make the job go smoothly is time well spent.

Before you start a project, make sure you have the right tools. Buy or rent those you don't have. Small tools, such as hammers and floats, are relatively inexpensive, so buy the best you can afford. Some inexpensive tools can wear out in the middle of the project.

Schedule delivery of all your materials and plan how you will store them, if necessary.

Finally, prepare yourself for the project. Read through the instructions completely before beginning. Plan every aspect of the project and make checklists, flowcharts, or schedules to help you keep everything in order. Be sure you are in good enough physical condition to do the work. Enlist helpers—friends make the job more enjoyable.

## WHEELBARROW RUNWAYS

Storing materials away from the job site poses a problem—how to get them from the storage area to the path. Wheelbarrows are the frequent answer, but these one-wheeled assistants can really tear up your yard.

To reduce the damage and avoid having to repair the wheelbarrow path, lay 2×10 or 2×12 planks to form a runway from storage to work site.

# NATURAL MATERIALS AND GRASS

Natural materials and grass make pleasant pathways through woodland or prairie settings and are among the easiest and least costly of paths to construct.

## NATURAL-MATERIAL PATHS

Water is the main enemy of a natural-material path. A site with insufficient drainage will get muddy, and the path materials will quickly decompose. Building the base properly will prevent water damage.

*Natural paths need periodic raking and retopping. Make grade changes with steps of stone or wood—natural surface materials erode quickly on steep slopes.*

■ Lay out your path as described in the previous chapter. Make sure your measurements include the width of any edging materials and forms. Remove the sod and excavate to a depth of at least 9 inches. This depth will accommodate a 4-inch gravel base, 3 inches of bark mulch for support, and 2 inches of topping material.

If your soil drains poorly, increase the excavation depth to 11 inches, then put in a 6-inch gravel base. If the path runs across boggy soil, add a 4-inch drainpipe in the gravel (see page 61).

■ Pour in and tamp the gravel so your edging is about ½ inch above grade, lay in a layer of landscape fabric, and set the edging on top of it.

■ Spread and tamp 3 inches of bark mulch to provide a foundation bed for the topping materials.

■ Spread and level 2 to 3 inches of pine needles, bark chips, or other topping materials. Tamp this layer down with your feet, and add more if necessary.

Natural materials will decompose, and you will need to replenish them. Most of them make an excellent mulch in the garden too.

## TOOLBOX

- Stakes, mason's line, 4-foot level
- Wheelbarrow
- Round- and square-nose shovels or spades
- Pitchfork (optional)
- Garden rake
- Leaf rake
- Tamper
- Level
- Tape measure
- Scissors (for cutting landscape fabric)

## MAKING A NATURAL-MATERIAL PATH

Outline path edges with marking spray paint, dig out original surface.

Place edging, pour in base material.

Spread topping material.

## GRASS PATHS

Grass paths don't require a base, and the simplest form requires only mowing. To mow a path, mark the centerline—tramp it down or chalk it. Mow low, in as many passes as the width requires.

Another simple technique involves cutting planting beds from the existing lawn. Visualize the lawn in reverse, marking out the areas that will remain as paths, (including any existing beds you want to reshape). Cut along the outline with an edging tool and remove the sod from beds.

New sod or seeded paths take a little more work.

## SOD AND SEEDED PATHS

**PREPARATION, SOD OR SEEDED:**
Break the surface and till 2 to 3 inches deep to loosen the soil. Break up clumps with a garden rake. Rake in starter fertilizer and soil amendments as needed for your area.

**FOR A SOD PATH:** Moisten dry soil and, starting at one end of the path, set sod strips firmly—lift up edges of adjoining pieces, pull them together, and push them down in the soil. Lay sod at right angles to slopes and pin the strips with sod staples. Roll the sod and water deeply. Hot weather requires three or more soakings per week

**FOR A SEEDED PATH:** Sow seed at recommended coverage rate. Lightly rake seed into top ¼ inch of soil. Roll path lightly. Mulch lightly, water, and mow when new growth is 2 to 3 inches high.

### TOOLBOX

- Stakes, mason's line, 4-foot level
- Wheelbarrow
- Round- and square-nose shovels or spades
- Garden rake
- Tamper
- Level
- Hose and sprinkler

**FOR A CUT PATH:**
- Lawn mower
- Edging tool

**FOR A SOD PATH:**
- Sod hatchet
- Kneeling board
- Sod staples for slopes
- Roller
- Tiller

**FOR A SEEDED PATH:**
- Hand or wheeled seeder
- Roller
- Tiller

*One of the easiest ways to make a grass path is to cut away the existing lawn and plant flower beds. Plan the path on paper first.*

**MAKING A SOD PATH**

Dig out original surface.

Till path area.

Roll out sod.

# LOOSE-STONE PATHS

*Loose stone crunches underfoot, making every stroll along it feel like a walk in the country. Aggregates are naturals in everything from rustic woodland settings to formal gardens.*

You may be tempted to lay loose stone directly on well-drained soil. However, your path will feel more solid underfoot, require less maintenance, and last longer without drainage problems if you lay it on a prepared base.

## BUILDING THE BASE

Excavation depth for the path depends on how well your soil drains. If you haven't tested your soil already, refer to page 16 for information on how to do it.

**LAYING OUT THE PATH:** Lay out the contours of your path, using batter boards or stakes for a straight design or garden hose for a curved installation. Be sure to include the width of the edging materials and any forms used to keep the edging straight. Mark the lines with spray marking paint, remove the sod, and excavate.

**HOW DEEP TO DIG?** If your soil drains rapidly, you can build the path on a 4-inch gravel base. In poorly draining soil, you'll need 6 inches of gravel. In heavy clays, excavate deep enough to install a drainpipe (see page 61).

**INSTALL EDGING FORMS:** If you are using forms, set them now. You can preassemble the forms from 2× stock and stakes, or drive the stakes first and then screw the forms to them (see page 56). In either case, stake the forms every 3 to 4 feet.

The soil determines whether to drive the stakes separately. Driving preassembled forms into clay soil is often difficult—stakes adjacent to the one you're driving hang up on the surface, increasing the probability of splitting the form board.

**ADDING THE GRAVEL BASE:** Shovel in gravel for the base and spread it with a garden rake. Gravel is hard to push around, so you need a sturdy rake. And it will spread more easily if you use the back side of the rake instead of the tines.

Build the gravel base a little at a time, tamping it about every 2 inches of depth. Make sure the base is level in all directions and along the length of the path. Scoop up or rake out gravel from high spots and add it to low spots.

**SET THE EDGING:** When you have about 4 inches of gravel in the base, set the edging material on the gravel to check the base height. Add to the base if necessary to bring the top of the edging to grade level, or higher if your plans call for it.

If the edging is already too high, use the side of the garden rake to scrape a trench in the base. Repeat either process until the edging is flush along the path surface.

**LAY IN LANDSCAPE FABRIC:** Cut landscape fabric so it fits snugly between the

## EDGES WITHOUT EDGING

If you want a loose-stone path without hard edging—to let loose materials edge a perennial bed, for instance—cut your landscape fabric wide enough to reach up the sides of the excavation.

These fabric ears will help keep the top layer out of the perennial bed. They will also keep the perennials from migrating into the path.

Loose materials will still wander out of the confines of the path. Keep them in place by making the path surface about 1 inch lower than the grade.

Setting the surface below grade means that water will flow more easily into the path. Unless the soil drains extremely fast, such installations need at least 6 inches of gravel so the path doesn't turn into a stream after a heavy rain.

## BUILDING A LOOSE-STONE PATH

Excavate.

Pour and tamp base material.

Pour and level surface material.

Set edging.

edges. (See "Edges Without Edging" on the opposite page.)

### TOPPING OFF THE PATH

Adding the top layer of loose stone will go more quickly than the base construction.
■ Pour the stone from a wheelbarrow or shovel it in with a round-nosed shovel. Shovel the stone into low areas and level it with the back of a garden rake, pushing and pulling the gravel to a consistent surface.
■ Dampen the surface with a fine spray and tamp it firmly. After tamping, add more stone, dampen it, and tamp again.

### KEEPING IT NEAT

Loose materials will move around with use, and materials on sloped paths will slide toward the bottom. To keep your path looking neat and orderly, rake it regularly. Start at the lower end of slopes and rake upward.

### ADD A SAND BASE

Loose stone should be ¾ inch or smaller for comfortable walking. But small sizes of sharp rock, such as crushed granite and quartz, may punch holes in the landscape fabric and migrate into the base.

Put a layer of sand on top of the landscape fabric to protect it. An inch or so of fine washed sand will compact and reduce the downward migration of your surface materials.

Be sure to include this layer when you figure the depth of your excavation.

### PLANTING IN LOOSE STONE

Plants in the path add colorful accents or textural contrast to loose-stone paths. To plant in loose stone:
■ Dig the surface and base materials all the way to the soil below. Cut the landscape fabric in an × and pull it aside. Enlarge the hole until it's about 4 inches wider than the nursery container.
■ Fill the hole with 3 to 4 inches of planting soil or compost.
■ Tease out the roots from the plant and set it in the soil slightly below the surface.
■ Fill the hole with planting soil and firm it. Push loose stones under the leaves, then water.

# FLAGSTONE PATHS

*Flagstone's varied textures and sizes go well with almost any design scheme. The flat stones can be arranged as stepping-stones or laid as a solid surface.*

Y ou can set individual flagstones in the soil in a stepping-stone pattern or lay them in a solid surface, either in sand or mortared to a slab. Setting stepping-stones is the easiest, but it's still heavy work.

## SETTING STEPPING-STONES

Stepping-stones do not require a gravel base, unless bedded in a loose-stone path (see page 72) or set in soil subject to extreme frost. (In climates with severe winters, prepare a gravel and sand base as shown on page 76, lay the stones, and backfill soil between them.)

You can set stepping-stones directly on the soil, but adding 1 to 2 inches of sand under each one will help them drain and minimize settling. Here's how to set them:

**LAYOUT:** Outline the path with two lengths of hose. Stepping-stones look good when arranged informally, but keep your contours from looking sloppy with 2×4 spacers (see page 53). Mark the lines with a light flour dusting along the hoses. (Paint will take longer to wear off.)

**SPACING:** Even though no two stones are alike, space them regularly to make walking easier. Placing them 6 inches apart will slow

**BUILDING A STEPPING-STONE PATH**

3. Set the stone in the recess and check it for level.

2. Use a round-nosed shovel to dig out the edges at the chalk. Remove the soil and shovel in 2" of sand.

4. Take up the stone and remove or add sand to make it level.

1. Lay out the individual stones in the pattern of your choice. Mark the outline of each stone with chalk. Remove the stone and set it aside.

## TOOLBOX

- Stakes, mason's line, 4-foot level
- Wheelbarrow
- Round- and square-nose shovels or spades
- Garden rake
- Tamper
- Level
- Saw (optional for cutting drainpipe)
- Scissors (for cutting landscape fabric)
- Tape measure
- Cordless drill (optional)
- Hammer
- Garden hose

**FOR MORTARED PATHS:**
- Tools for installing concrete
- Mortar box
- Pointed and straight trowels
- Mortar bag

**STONE-CUTTING TOOLS:**
- Stonemason's hammer
- Small sledge
- Cold-steel chisels
- Wedges
- Masonry saw

down the pace and let the walker admire your planting beds. On a functional walk, use 10-inch spacing to speed traffic. For a utility path that you'll wheel garden equipment over, leave 1 to 2 inches between stones. Set the stones out and walk on them to make sure the spacing feels comfortable.

**CHALK THE LOCATION:** When you're sure of your layout, outline each stone with powdered chalk (the kind used for chalk lines). Cut the tip of the container about ⅜ inch from the top, and squeeze the bottle to expel the chalk.

**PREPARE THE RECESS:** Set each stone aside and dig out along the chalked line. Remove the sod and excavate so the stone will sit low enough to run the lawn mower over when set in 1 to 2 inches of sand. Tamp the soil with the end of a 2×4.

**ADD THE SAND BASE:** Using a round-nosed shovel, add 1 to 2 inches of sand to the recess. The sand conforms to irregularities on the bottom of the stone so it will sit level at the correct height. Set all the stones roughly in the first pass, then go back and level them.

**LEVELING THE STONES:** Using a level wide enough to span the largest stone, level each one, keeping the stones low enough for lawn mowing. Check each stone for level in several directions.

Pull the stone out and add or remove sand with a trowel as necessary to make fine adjustments. Lay a piece of 2×4 on each stone and tap it lightly with a small sledge. The 2×4 prevents you from cracking a stone.

## STEPPING-STONE LAYOUT TIPS

Here are ideas for your stepping-stone design:
■ Stepping-stones are usually a one-person path, so you can keep the scale small.
■ To start and stop the path or signal changes of direction, use stones about 1½ times larger than average. Lay these junction stones first.
■ Try to pattern the stones so their contours relate to each other (see illustration, right).
■ Lay long stones across the path, not parallel with its direction.
■ Stones with recesses will collect water, which can freeze, become dangerous, and split the stone. Select stones with flat surfaces.
■ Stones equal in thickness will make installation much easier. Stepping-stones should be at least 1½ inches thick. Thin stones break easily under very little weight.

## DESIGNING A STONE SURFACE

The infinite variety of natural flagstone lends itself to stunning layouts but can also leave you overwhelmed with design possibilities.

**PLANTING STEPPING-STONE GAPS**

1. Remove just enough soil to accommodate the root of the plant.

2. Set the plug into the soil and press additional soil around it gently.

3. Dampen the soil.

For both dry-laid and mortared flagstone surfaces, make things easier by laying a trial pattern off to the side of the site.

Start by sorting the stones into piles according to size. Begin your trial pattern at the path edges, selecting larger stones with straight sides. Vary the sizes of these edge stones and leave some for the interior as well. This will keep the pattern interesting. Try to arrange the contours of the stones so they mirror each other, fitting the concave edge of one stone near the convex side of the other. When you are satisfied with your design, you can set the stones in the same order, either on sand or mortar.

## GETTING THE DESIGN RIGHT

Wherever possible, choose adjoining stones with contours that mate.

Experiment to get the best design when laying a flagstone surface. Lay the stones out at the side of the path. Set them on tarps to avoid damaging the lawn. (Don't leave the tarp too long or you'll kill the grass.)

First select larger stones with straight sides for the path edge. Then set smaller stones, placing similar contours next to each other. Cut the edges to get the right shape, if necessary. Stand back and view your work. Then adjust the layout as needed, and move the stones sequentially into their locations on the path.

# FLAGSTONE PATHS
*continued*

## SETTING FLAGSTONE IN SAND

The naturally uneven edges of flagstone prohibit you from spacing them consistently on the path, but try to set them about ½ inch or less from each other. More sand will tend to work its way out of a wider gap.

**BUILD THE BASE:** Lay out the path using the techniques shown on the previous page. Excavate to a depth that will accommodate the materials and leave the paving about ½ inch above grade. Add 4 to 6 inches of gravel depending on drainage requirements. Level and tamp the base. Cut and lay landscape fabric on the gravel and set the edging, if you are using it.

**LAY THE SAND BED:** Shovel in and spread about 2 inches of washed sand. Dampen the sand, screed it level, and tamp it.

**SET THE STONES:** Begin with the edge stones first, transferring them from your trial layout. Fill in the gaps with smaller stones.

Push and rock the stones into the sand bed as you lay them. After you have set a 3- to 4-foot section, check it for level. Pull up stones that aren't level, removing or adding sand as necessary.

Set the stones by tapping them with a small sledge (protect the stone surface with a scrap of 2×4). Continue setting the stones in sections, making the surface of each section level with the previous one. Smooth stones will level easily. You can check several sections at a time by placing the level on an 8-foot 2×4. Leveling rough stones by eye is usually adequate.

**FILL THE GAPS:** Shovel sand between the joints, and sweep it across the surface with a push broom until it nearly fills the joint. Then dampen it. Top off the joints by sweeping in sand from all directions. Repeat this process until the sand in the joints is ¼ to ⅛ inch below the surface of the stones. That small recess will reduce the amount of sand displaced—or tracked into the house.

## SETTING FLAGSTONE IN SAND

7. Sweep sand into gaps.

6. Check each stone for level as you go.

5. Set stone by tapping in place.

4. Lay flagstone.

3. Spread sand, dampen, and tamp.

2. Pour and level gravel base.

1. Excavate to the depth required by the thickness of materials.

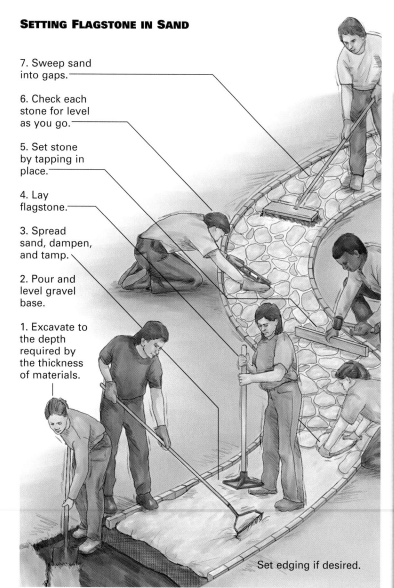

Set edging if desired.

## CUTTING NATURAL STONE

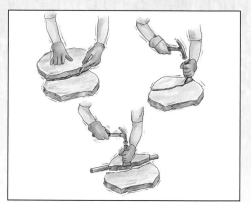

You can cut flagstone to fit your path or to conform to the edges of other stone when nature (or the stone yard) doesn't supply the right shapes.

■ First mark the stone to be cut. Use a carpenter's pencil or welder's chalk. Set an adjoining stone on top if cutting to match contours.

■ Next place a mason's chisel on the line and strike the chisel sharply with a small sledge.

■ Lay the stone on a pipe or another stone and strike the line again to break off the waste.

■ You may be able to trim the edges of thin flagstone by chipping the edge with a mason's hammer.

## THE MORTARED-STONE PATH

Mortared flagstone requires a solid concrete base. Refer to the information on pages 64–67 when building a mortared path. Joint spacing is a matter of preference, but ¾-inch joints look good and are easy to mortar.

**BUILD THE BASE:** Lay out the path. Excavate to a depth that will accommodate the gravel base, the concrete slab, and the thickness of your flagstone. Build forms for the slab and shovel in 4 to 6 inches of gravel. Level and tamp the gravel. Lay in reinforcing wire mesh supported on dobies.

**POUR THE SLAB:** Bring concrete to the site in wheelbarrows or by truck. Pour the concrete between the forms. Spread it with shovels and make sure it fills the forms.

**SCREED AND FLOAT THE SLAB:** Pull a screed board across the surface of the concrete to level it. Repeat the screeding after filling any depressions. Float the surface (see page 66) and broom-finish it. Let the concrete cure for three days to a week.

**MAKE MORTAR SCREED BOARDS (OPTIONAL):** You can spread mortar to its proper depth without screed boards, leveling the stones as you go, but screeding the mortar will make the bed depth more consistent. Fasten 2×4s to stakes (keep the tops of the stakes flush with the top edges of the 2×4s). Set these preassembled guides on top of the slab forms. Toenail the screed guides to the forms.

**SPREAD THE MORTAR BED:** Mix enough type M mortar (for outdoor use) to cover an area you can set in about 10 minutes. Using a square trowel, spread a 2-inch mortar bed. Then if you've installed screed guides, screed each section with a 2×4 notched 1½ inches deep at both ends. The notched 2×4 will spread the mortar evenly 2 inches deep.

**SET THE PAVING:** Bring each stone from the test site and push (don't slide) it gently into the mortar. Continue setting stones until you have finished the section, then lay a level on the section and adjust any stones that are too high or too low. Tap each stone with a small sledge and a 2×4.

### SCREEDING MORTAR

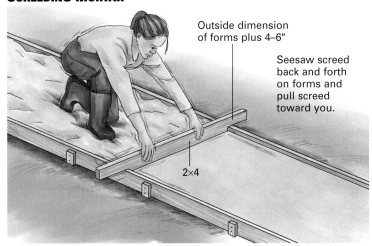

Outside dimension of forms plus 4–6"

Seesaw screed back and forth on forms and pull screed toward you.

2×4

Continue setting stones until you've covered the entire path. Let the installation set up overnight.

**MORTAR THE STONES:** A mortar bag makes it easy to put the mortar in the joints, not on the stones. Squeeze the bag to push the mortar into the joints, cleaning off any spillage immediately. When the mortar will hold a thumbprint, smooth it with a pointing tool. Let the mortar cure.

### INSTALLING A MORTARED FLAGSTONE PATH

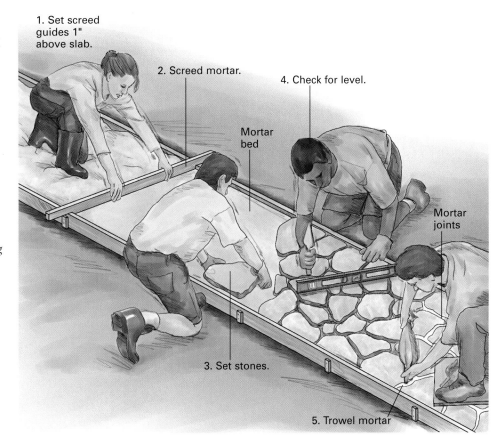

1. Set screed guides 1" above slab.

2. Screed mortar.

4. Check for level.

Mortar bed

Mortar joints

3. Set stones.

5. Trowel mortar

# CUT-STONE PATHS

Cut stone comes from the same natural rock as flagstone and lends itself to the same kind of sand-bed and mortared installations.

Because of their regular shapes, however, you can lay out cut-stone patterns on paper before setting them. You may need to make minor adjustments as you lay the stones, but plans on paper will save you from having to conduct major experiments on site.

*With its regular shape, cut stone suits formal settings. Even in such installations, however, the texture of the path will vary because no two stones are identical. Cut stone is perfect for designs in which you want variety within a uniform design.*

## CUT-STONE SETTINGS

Whether you fill the joints between cut stones with sand or mortar depends in part on how you want the finished path to look and how the edges of your stone are cut.

Stone cut with precise edges, such as stone tile, looks best with narrow joints—about $1/16$ inch. Mortar is too thick for such narrow joints, but you can still mortar the pieces to a slab and finish the joints with fine sand. (See page 77 for information about mortaring stones to a slab.) You can also set the stone in a sand bed and finish the joints with sand.

Most cut stone looks better finished with sand because close spacing enhances the pattern. If you do make mortar joints, space

the stones no closer than $3/8$ inch and consider using mortar tinted to closely match the color of the stone. You can also set cut stone as individual stepping-stones, following the same procedures used for flagstone (see page 74).

## SETTING CUT STONE IN SAND

Sand-laid cut stone requires a solid base and a level sand bed.

**BUILD THE BASE:** Lay out the path and excavate to a depth that will put the paving surface about $1/2$ inch above grade. Add 4 to 6 inches of gravel for the base, depending on drainage requirements for your soil. Level and tamp the gravel. Cut landscape fabric to size, lay it on the gravel base, and position the edging, if you are using any.

If the path runs along a perennial bed, consider setting cut stones on edge to create a low border along your path. Setting these stones tightly together will help keep soil in the bed from spreading onto the path.

**LAY THE SAND BED:** Shovel in and spread about 2 inches of washed sand. Dampen the sand, screed it level, and tamp it.

**SET THE STONES:** Cut stone is rarely

## TOOLBOX

- Stakes, mason's line, 4-foot level
- Wheelbarrow
- Round- and square-nose shovels or spades
- Garden rake
- Tamper
- Level
- Saw (optional for cutting drainpipe)
- Scissors (for cutting landscape fabric)
- Tape measure
- Cordless drill (optional)
- Hammer
- Push broom

### FOR MORTARED PATHS:
- Tools for installing concrete
- Mortar box
- Pointed and straight trowels
- Mortar bag

### STONE-CUTTING TOOLS:
- Stonemason's hammer
- Small sledge
- Cold-steel chisels
- Wedges
- Masonry saw

produced in identical sizes and shapes, so try to lay them with an average spacing that will look consistent over the course of the path.

Arrange the stones in sections, following your dimensioned plan. For narrow spacing, keep the stones ¼ to ⅜ inch apart. Your path will look tightly laid if the average spacing doesn't exceed ½ inch. Larger gaps can cause the sand to migrate out of the joints and be tracked into your house.

When you have the spacing correct, push and rock the stones down into the sand bed. Check them for level in several directions with a 4-foot level. Pull up stones that deviate from level, and remove or add sand as necessary to level them.

Tap the stones with a small sledge (protect the stone with a piece of 2×4) to set them. Continue setting the stones in sections, making sure the surface of each section lies flush with the previous ones. Place the 4-foot level in the middle of an 8-foot 2×4 to check several sections at once.

**FILL THE GAPS:** Shovel sand between the joints and brush it between the stones with a push broom. When sand nearly fills the joint, dampen it. Top off the joints by sweeping in more sand from all directions, leaving the sand ⅛ to ¼ inch below the top of the stones. That small recess will reduce the amount of sand displaced or tracked into the house. Repeat this process for all joints.

**SETTING CUT STONE IN SAND**

1. Excavate to the depth required by the thickness of materials.

2. Pour and level gravel base.

3. Spread sand, dampen, and tamp.

4. Set edging if desired.

5. Lay cut-stone paving.

6. Set stone by tapping into place.

7. Check each stone for level as you go.

8. Sweep sand into gaps.

## CUTTING TO FIT

Cut stone comes from the quarry or stone yard cut into regular shapes with straight edges, but your path layout will probably require that you cut some of them.

Soft stone, such as bluestone, limestone, or sandstone, will fracture cleanly along a scored line. If your stones are thin (1½ inches or less), use the same techniques shown on page 76 for cutting flagstone, scoring it gently with a mason's chisel and tapping the stone on the outside of the scored line.

If you're working with harder stone or have a lot of cuts to make, rent a masonry saw. These tools come in a variety of styles, but one feature is consistent to all of them—they use water to cool the blade. Don't make cuts, even small ones, without cooling water for the blade.

Wear eye and ear protection when cutting. Mark the cut line with a straightedge, set the stone on the saw table, and turn the saw on. For stone up to 1 inch thick, you can cut through. For thicker stone, set the saw to score the stone about ½ inch deep. Then lay the stone on a 2×4 with the scored line at the edge of the board and tap the outside edge with a mason's hammer to snap the stone.

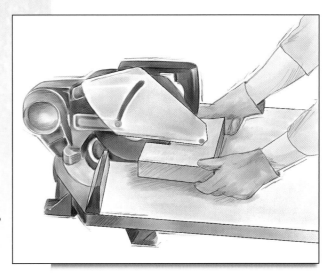

# BRICK PATHS

*If you're looking for a classic path design, brick is the natural choice. Edging helps hold unmortared bricks in place.*

Brick paths often look complicated because of their patterns, but they are no more difficult to build than any other hard-surface path. They usually take more time to lay because the bricks are small and the patterns require some precision.

Set up a mock section (see "Design Tips" on page 35) and measure it, allowing for mortar joints, edging, and the width of forms. Set your layout stakes exactly to this width.

## SETTING BRICK IN SAND

Like other materials, sand-laid brick calls for a solid base and a level sand bed.
**BUILD THE BASE:** Lay out the path using the techniques shown on page 52, and excavate to a depth that will accommodate the materials and leave the paving about ½ inch above grade. Add ¼ inch if you plan to crown the surface to improve drainage. Add 4 to 6 inches of gravel, depending on drainage requirements for your soil (see page

16), and level and tamp the gravel. Cut landscape fabric and lay it on the gravel. Then set the edging on the fabric.
**LAY THE SAND BED:** Shovel in and spread about 2 inches of washed sand. Dampen the sand, screed it level, and tamp it.
**SET THE BRICK:** Brick has to be set precisely. Tie a mason's line to stakes on either side of the path as a guide, or tie the line to bricks (shown in the illustration below) to make the line easier to move.

Space the path bricks ⅛ inch apart and check each course with a straightedge before laying the next one. You can place ⅛-inch wooden spacers between the bricks, but make sure they are long enough to retrieve easily.

Beginning in one corner, push each brick straight down into the sand. Continue until you have laid about a 4-foot section, supporting your weight on 2-foot plywood

### ALIGNING A BRICK SETTING

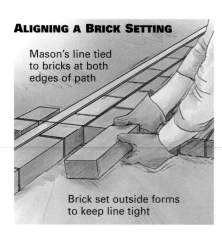

Mason's line tied to bricks at both edges of path

Brick set outside forms to keep line tight

### LEVELING BRICK

Check for level, and set brick with rubber mallet.

### SWEEPING IN THE SAND

Sweep sand into joints from all directions.

**LAYING BRICKS IN SAND**

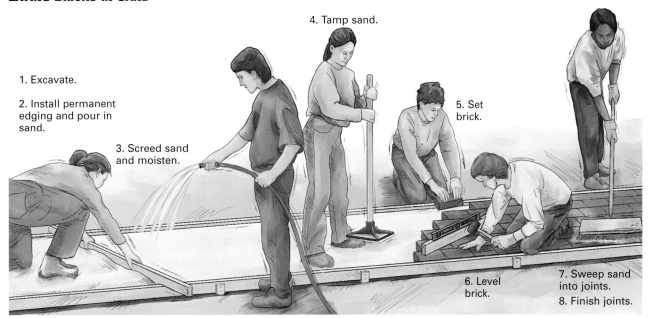

1. Excavate.

2. Install permanent edging and pour in sand.

3. Screed sand and moisten.

4. Tamp sand.

5. Set brick.

6. Level brick.

7. Sweep sand into joints.

8. Finish joints.

squares. Check the section in several directions with a 4-foot level. Pull up bricks if necessary, digging out or adding sand. Set each brick by tapping it with a rubber mallet. **FILL THE GAPS:** You can fill all the joints when the path is complete or fill them in sections. If you have used spacers, fill the gaps in sections so you can reuse the spacers.

Shovel sand into the joints, and brush it with a push broom. When it nearly fills the joints, dampen it. Sweep in more sand from all directions, leaving the sand about ⅛ inch below the surface, or at the bottom of the chamfer for chamfered brick.

## LAYOUT PATTERNS

When choosing brick patterns (also called their *bond*), consider the aesthetic effect, the relation of the path to its surroundings, how long the pattern will take to lay, and how many bricks you'll have to cut.

The jack-on-jack pattern is the simplest to lay, but is the least interesting. However, if you lay out your path to conform exactly to the width of the pattern, you won't have to cut any brick.

Patterns increase in appeal as they become more complex. You'll have to cut bricks for some patterns.

A running bond will hide any small variations in the sizes of the brick. The herringbone pattern looks best when it can spread out—on walks at least 3 feet wide. Narrow paths make the pattern seem too busy. The basket weave and its half-weave cousin are best set with modular brick.

# BRICK PATHS
*continued*

## BUILDING A MORTARED-BRICK PATH

Mortared brick on a slab, like other mortared paths, requires that you build what amounts to two walks—the concrete base for the brick and the paving layer itself. All this work will pay off with a path that will last for years.

**BUILD THE BASE:** Lay out the path. Excavate to a depth that will accommodate the gravel base, the concrete slab, and the thickness of the brick—a total of 10 to 12 inches, probably. Build forms for the slab and shovel in 4 to 6 inches of gravel. Level and tamp the gravel. Lay in reinforcing wire mesh tied to dobies.

**POUR THE SLAB:** Bring concrete to the site in wheelbarrows or by truck. Pour the concrete between the forms, spreading it with shovels and making sure it fills all recesses.

**SCREED AND FLOAT THE SLAB:** Pull a screed across the surface of the concrete to level it, repeating the screeding after filling in any depressions. Float the surface (see page 66) and broom-finish it. Let the concrete cure for three days to a week.

**MAKE SCREED BOARDS (OPTIONAL):** You can spread mortar to its proper depth without screed boards, leveling the brick as you go, but screeding the mortar will make the bed depth more consistent. Rip 2×4s to a width equal to the combined thickness of the mortar bed and brick—usually about 3 inches. Screw the ripped boards to stakes (keep the stakes flush with the top edge of the boards) and place the preassembled guides on top of the slab forms. Toenail the screed guides to the forms.

**SPREAD THE MORTAR BED:** Mix enough type M mortar (for outdoor use) to cover an area about 4×4 feet, or a space you can set in about 30 minutes. Consider the weather when calculating your setting area. In hot weather, mortar may start setting up in as few as 15 minutes. Using a square trowel, spread a mortar bed about ½ inch thick. If you've installed 3-inch screed boards, screed each section with a 2×4 notched 2½ inches deep at both ends to spread the mortar evenly ½ inch thick.

**SET THE PAVING:** Before you start, wet the brick with a hose so it won't draw moisture from the mortar. Then tie mason's lines to two bricks and set them outside the screed guides. The mason's lines will help you keep the bricks straight and level.

Start in a corner, and working in square or triangular sections—depending on your pattern—push each brick straight down into the mortar. Then tap it with the handle of a pointed trowel. Insert spacers between the bricks as you lay them, checking the rows with a straightedge.

Continue laying the brick until you have finished a section. Then lay a level on the section and adjust any bricks that are too high

## SETTING BRICK IN A MORTAR BED

Level

⅜" spacers

Mason's line

Tap brick level with trowel.

## GROUTING MORTARED BRICK

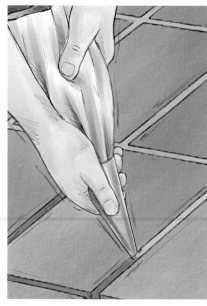

Squeeze mortar from bag as you fill joints. Keep tip in contact with brick.

## BUILDING A MORTARED-BRICK PATH

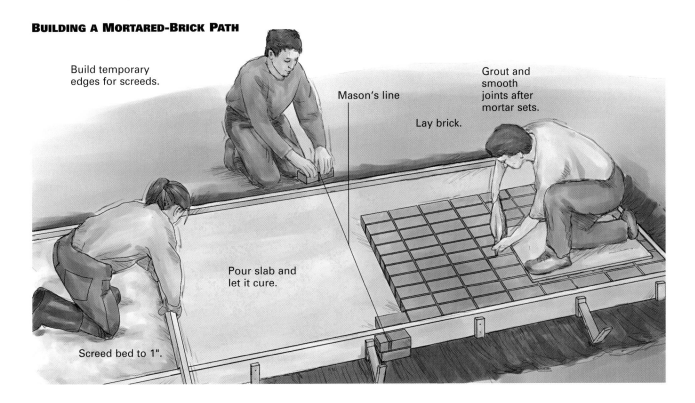

Build temporary edges for screeds.

Mason's line

Grout and smooth joints after mortar sets.

Lay brick.

Pour slab and let it cure.

Screed bed to 1".

or too low. Tap high bricks with a rubber mallet. Pull up low bricks, add mortar, and tap them level. To make sure all the sections are level, set an 8-foot 2×4 on edge and sight along the bottom, looking for gaps. Continue laying brick, moving the mason's line and checking the rows with a straightedge, until you've covered the entire path. Let the mortar set up overnight.

**MORTAR THE BRICKS:** It's easier to put mortar into the joints with a mortar bag than with a pointed trowel. Squeeze the bag to push the mortar into the joints, cleaning off any spillage immediately.

When the mortar will hold a thumbprint, smooth it with a pointing tool. Let the mortar cure for three or four days.

### TILING A WALK

The surface of the slab for a tiled walk must be flat. Tile is great for dressing up an old slab, but check the structural integrity of the slab first. Lay a long 2×4 across the surface—dips or humps should be no more than $\frac{1}{8}$ inch for every 10 feet. Grind down high spots with a carbide grinder and fill in depressions with self-leveling compound. Clean the slab with a solution of 1 cup trisodium phosphate in a gallon of water.

Spread a smooth $\frac{1}{4}$-inch bond coat of latex-cement mortar and let it dry. Then trowel on a $\frac{1}{2}$-inch coat with a notched trowel, and set the tile in sections. Use spacers and follow the techniques for setting brick. Grout the tiles after the mortar sets.

### CUTTING BRICK

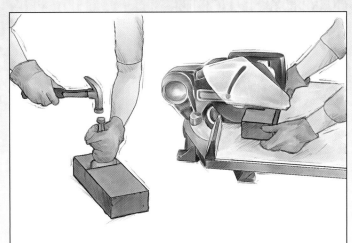

You may not have to cut any bricks for patterns set in straight, formal lines. Curved paths and patterns such as the half basket weave will require cutting. Use a brick set and heavy hammer to score a line on all four sides of the brick, then center the brick set in the line and rap it sharply. The brick will cleave neatly along the line. If you have a lot of brick to cut, rent a masonry saw. If many bricks need to be cut to the same size, do the cutting all at once to reduce rental time.

# PRECAST PAVERS

Precast pavers are made for the do-it-yourselfer. Uniform shapes and repeating patterns make layout and design decisions easy. Interlocking edges make pavers perfect for sand-bed projects, and uniform sizes make them easy to estimate. Easy-to-install preformed plastic edging keeps them in place and isn't visible after backfilling.

## SETTING PRECAST PAVERS

Like other materials, pavers need a well-drained base and a level sand bed.

**BUILD THE BASE:** Lay out the path. If you're using plastic edging, be sure to include its width in the layout and allow enough room to drive the anchor pins into the soil. Excavate to a depth that will accommodate the materials and leave the paving about ½ inch above grade. Add 4 to 6 inches of gravel, depending on how well your soil drains (see page 16). Level and tamp the gravel. Cut landscape fabric and lay it on

*Precast pavers are easy to install, but choose the pattern carefully. Make sure the scale of the pattern suits your landscape.*

the gravel. Install any other type of edging on the fabric.

**LAY THE SAND BED:** Shovel in and spread about 2 inches of washed sand. Dampen the sand, screed it level, and tamp it.

**SET THE PAVERS:** Pavers must be set precisely, and interlocking edges on many styles make this easy. Some have integral lugs that keep the pavers aligned and spaced.

Starting in a corner, lay the first few pavers snugly against the edging. Tap each block with a rubber mallet to set it firmly into the sand. Push the next rows of pavers against each other, spacing unlugged pavers with ⅛-inch plywood strips. As you lay the pavers, work in two directions to keep your design from shifting to either side. Every few courses, lay a carpenter's level or a long, straight 2×4 across the surface to make sure the pavers are at a consistent height.

It's almost impossible to avoid high and low spots. To adjust pavers, remove several from the area, remove or add sand as necessary, and reset the pavers. It's best to check the surface as you set each row because pavers fit tightly and can be difficult to remove. To remove a stubborn paver, pry it from opposite sides at the same time with two straight screwdrivers gripping the sides about ¼ inch below the surface.

**CUTTING PAVERS:** Precast pavers are made of concrete, and concrete won't fracture cleanly like brick. Use a masonry saw to cut pavers.

**FILL THE GAPS:** Fill joints in the path with sand. You can fill them in sections or wait until you complete the entire path. Shovel sand between the joints, brushing it with a push broom. When it nearly fills the joint, dampen it. Top off the joints by sweeping in more sand from all directions, leaving it about ⅛ inch below the surface or at the bottom of the chamfer on chamfered pavers.

## SETTING PRECAST PAVERS

## FINISHING THE SURFACE

Check the surface for level.

Tap pavers into place with a rubber mallet.

Set cut pavers at the edge as you install the field pattern. If you set the edges last, the paver may not fit the recess.

Sweep sand into joints from all directions.

## BUILDING A PATH WITH PRECAST PAVERS

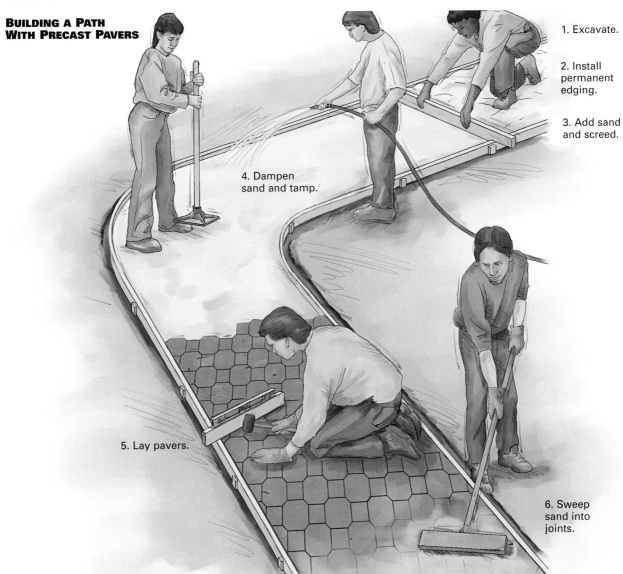

1. Excavate.

2. Install permanent edging.

3. Add sand and screed.

4. Dampen sand and tamp.

5. Lay pavers.

6. Sweep sand into joints.

# WOOD PATHS

*A boardwalk and a wood bridge look distinctive in this garden. Naturally resistant wood species or pressure-treated lumber are necessary in ground contact.*

Basic carpentry skills and a few tools are all you need to install a small wood walk in a weekend. Longer walks might take more time, but most of your effort will be spent on the preparation of the base.

Wood walks (or boardwalks) need drainage—perhaps more than any other type of path—because wood is subject to decay and damage by the elements. Choose naturally resistant woods (see page 38) or pressure-treated lumber rated for ground contact.

Decking sizes vary with individual designs, from 2×6s to 2×8s or wider. Wider boards will cover the walk more quickly, but be careful to maintain a pleasing scale.

You can apply any exterior stain or finish to your wood either before or after installing it. If using brushed-on products, it's easier to prefinish the wood. Spray preservatives also should be applied before you build the walk. That way you can apply preservative on the underside of the decking.

## INSTALLING SLEEPERS

2×4

2" sand (optional)

4–6" gravel

2×4

## LAYING THE DECKING

Framing square

2×6s spaced ⅜" apart

## BUILDING A DECKED WALK

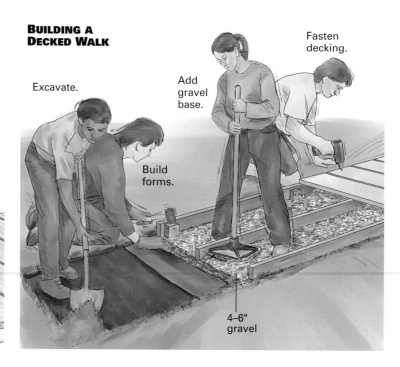

Excavate.

Build forms.

Add gravel base.

Fasten decking.

4–6" gravel

## BUILDING A WOOD WALK

The design shown here works well on generally flat ground. To accommodate small variations in grade, either alter the depth of the excavation or build small sections to avoid spanning changes in grade. Crossing a stream bed or deep gully might require building a section and supporting it at both ends and in the center with 4-inch posts set in soil or concrete.

**BUILD THE BASE:** Lay out the path. Excavate to a depth that will accommodate the gravel bed and leave the top of the decking at least 1½ inches above the ground.

Cut enough 18- to 20-inch 2×4 stakes so you can install them every 3 feet on both sides of the excavation. For walks 3 feet or wider, cut stakes for a center sleeper too. Point the stakes and drive them into the ground 1½ inches from the edge. For a center sleeper, locate the stakes so the sleeper will be centered in the path.

Restake mason's line, if necessary, to keep the lines straight. Make sure the stakes are the same height from the bottom of the excavation throughout. Add 4 inches of gravel and level and tamp it. Cut landscape fabric and lay it on the gravel, slitting the fabric at the stakes. Be sure the fabric extends the full width of the base.

**INSTALL THE SLEEPERS:** Cut 2×4s to lengths that will span each flat area on the path, and fasten them with 2½-inch treated deck screws driven through the stakes. Where two sleepers join, strengthen the joint with ¾-inch plywood on either side. Support the joint with a stake. Recheck the sleepers for level and make corrections if necessary.

**INSTALL THE DECKING:** Cut the decking to length. It can be long enough to span the width of the walk, or longer so it overhangs the sleepers by 1½ to 2 inches on either side. Using a cordless drill, fasten the decking to the sleepers with 3-inch treated deck screws, two screws into each sleeper. Except for pressure-treated stock, use plywood spacers to keep the boards consistently ¼ to ⅜ inch apart. Butt pressure-treated boards against each other—they will shrink as they dry out.

**APPLY THE FINISH:** If you haven't done so already, spray or brush on the finish.

## PREFAB PANELS

Prefab decking panels are made in a variety of patterns and will save you a lot of time when building a wood walk. They come at a higher cost, of course. Some have a ready-made, non-slip surface. Design your path to use available sizes.

## INSTALLING TIES AND TIMBERS

Railroad ties or large landscape timbers make attractive paths and steps that don't require much more than a strong back and a little ingenuity.
■ Arrange the timbers on the path in their approximate locations.
■ Move the timbers into their final location, spacing them evenly.
■ Outline each timber with marking chalk.
■ Remove timber and excavate to a depth that will leave its top edge about ½ to 1 inch above grade.
■ Tamp 1 inch of sand in the excavation.
■ Set timber on sand and level length and width.
■ Drive 18-inch lengths of ½-inch rebar through predrilled holes in the timber, flush with the top.

Flagstone or other material

½" rebar

## WALKING THE PLANKS

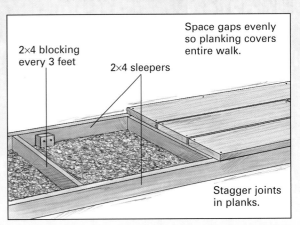

2×4 blocking every 3 feet

2×4 sleepers

Space gaps evenly so planking covers entire walk.

Stagger joints in planks.

Planks are installed parallel to the sleepers. A planked walk makes an attractive addition to the landscape on its own, and you can install planked sections to accent sections with decking. Begin construction with sleepers as you would a decked walk. Install 2×4 blocking every 3 feet across the path, fastening them with galvanized screws driven through the sleepers. Stagger the joints to make the walk stronger along its length and make sure to center the joints on the blocking.

# CONCRETE FOR PATHS

*Colored and patterned concrete makes this driveway durable and attractive. Concrete paths and sidewalks can be finished the same way. Many patterns are possible.*

## TOOLBOX

- Stakes, mason's line, 4-foot level, tape measure
- Wheelbarrow
- Round- and square- nose shovels or spades
- Garden rake
- Tamper
- Level
- Circular saw
- Cordless drill
- Hammer
- Mason's hoe
- Floating tools—float, bullfloat, darby, edger
- Finishing tools— steel trowel, stamping tools (will vary with design)

Concrete for small jobs—those requiring ¼ cubic yard of concrete or less—can be mixed in a wheelbarrow from premixed bags. A power mixer is useful when you need up to a cubic yard. But mixing and pouring concrete by hand for larger jobs is neither cost nor labor efficient.

No matter what size the job, prepare the surrounding lawn to minimize damage caused by concrete work. Lay 2×10 planks to make ramps for hauling bags of mix or the concrete itself across the lawn in a wheelbarrow. Extend the ramps up and over the forms so you can wheel the mix into them, as shown on page 90.

Mix the ingredients as close to the site as you can; buying a longer hose to get water to the mixing area is cheaper (and easier) than resodding a damaged strip of lawn. If you're using ready-mix, ask about pumping it so the driver doesn't have to drive the truck onto the yard.

### BUILDING THE BASE

**EXCAVATE:** Dig the path to a depth that will accommodate a 4- to 6-inch gravel base and 3 to 4 inches of concrete. Just how much of each material you need will depend on local conditions and how the surface will be used. Most walks hold up well with 3 inches of

reinforced concrete; a driveway needs to be thicker. Local building code officials can give you the specifications for your project.

**MAKE THE FORMS:** Install 2× forms, referring to the information on page 56. Drive stakes into the ground along the layout lines, setting them so they will be flush with or below the final form level. Let the stakes follow the contour of sloped ground. Then fasten the forms to the stakes with 2½-inch screws. If your forms will remain in place as permanent edging, the top edges will be visible. Mask the top edges with duct tape to keep the concrete from staining them.

Splice joints in the forms with ¾-inch plywood plates, and brace the splice with a diagonal stake. Install additional diagonal braces every 4 to 6 feet. The weight of the concrete and expansion as it cures can quickly dislodge forms if you don't brace them properly. Even slight bulges in the forms will show on your walk.

Remember that the height of the forms should be the same as the finished height of the slab. The forms not only contain the concrete, they also act as guides for screeding it level.

**ADD GRAVEL:** Bring gravel to the site by wheelbarrow, and spread it as level as possible with shovels and garden rakes. Then wet it down and pack it with a power tamper or a plate compactor. Do a thorough job, going over every spot at least twice. Repeat this process until the gravel is at the correct depth and feels solid.

**PUT IN REINFORCEMENT:** Set dobies on the gravel about every 2 to 3 feet and lay #10 6×6 reinforcing wire mesh in the forms. Tie the mesh to the dobies.

### POURING THE SLAB

Bring concrete to the site by wheelbarrow or truck. If you're pouring ready-mix, decide ahead of time which of your helpers will handle the chute (the truck operator often will do this), who will spread the concrete, who will consolidate it, and who will screed. The person running the chute signals the operator when to stop the flow of concrete. Concrete will continue to run out of the chute about 15 seconds after the flow stops.

If you're moving the mix from the truck or mixing area by wheelbarrow, don't try to horse the wheelbarrow around. Pick up the handles evenly, just enough to get the legs off the ground. Let momentum from the weight of the mix help you carry it to the site.

**POUR THE CONCRETE:** Fill the forms, working from the farthest end of the path to the mixing site. Pour the mix in piles next to each other, spreading it with shovels and making sure it fills all recesses. Try to get the piles about an inch higher than the forms so you won't have to move as much concrete to level it out. Work the concrete in sections of about 5 feet.

**SETTLE THE CONCRETE:** Consolidate, or settle, the concrete by jabbing a shovel or 2×4 up and down in it. Make sure the mesh stays centered, pulling it up with a garden rake, if necessary. Tamp the mix down at the corners and along the edges of the forms.

**SCREED THE SLAB:** Once you have filled a 5-foot section, pull a screed board—a straight 2x4—across the surface of the concrete to level it. Screeding is best done with two people seesawing the board back and forth, pulling it across the surface of the walk and keeping it in contact with the forms at all times. If the screed rides up over the concrete, back up a little and start again. Repeat the screeding after filling in any depressions.

## ASPHALT: HOT OR COLD?

Laying hot asphalt requires specialized heavy equipment and professional expertise. Cold-rolled asphalt doesn't demand nearly as much skill.

Cold-rolled asphalt, a semisoft petroleum product, can improve an existing slab by covering it. Buy it in bags (usually 50 pounds and more) at your home center. Fill holes and repair cracks in the surface and brush on a coat of bitumen emulsion to improve the adhesion. Spread the emulsion with an old garage brush and throw the brush away. Let the emulsion dry and pour out the asphalt. Spread it with a garden rake to a ¾-inch thickness, using the rake to break up the clumps. Then roll it with a garden roller, filling in any depressions with fresh asphalt and rolling again. Mist the roller with a hose or watering can so it doesn't pick up the material.

## BUILDING DRIVEWAYS

Building a driveway is a major undertaking. Make the job go smoothly by preparing everything properly and having enough help on hand.

Depending on the size of the project, you'll need from eight to ten people in good shape. It will help if at least three of them have had some previous experience with concrete work and can act as crew chiefs, accomplishing tasks as they need to be done. The other, less experienced members will catch on quickly.

When you've finished the preparation work, think of the project in sections. You should begin the pour at the end farthest from the ready-mix truck, and work toward it. The truck operator will extend the delivery chute or pump hose to that location and will expect to have some of your workers move the concrete with shovels, tamp it into the corners, and level that section. All of these activities will continue as you begin the next section; your second crew needs to be ready to do the same things there. Continue pouring and working in sections, and rotate the first group to the poured area when necessary. When you've finished the pour, each group can work on floating the sections individually.

# CONCRETE FOR PATHS
*continued*

## BUILDING A CONCRETE WALK

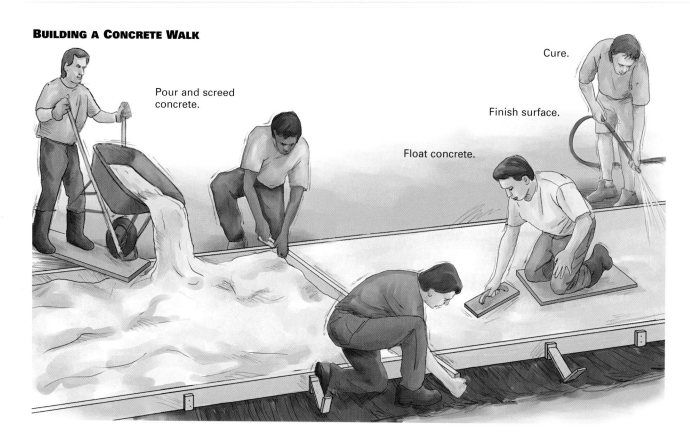

Pour and screed concrete.

Float concrete.

Finish surface.

Cure.

## EDGING AND JOINTING

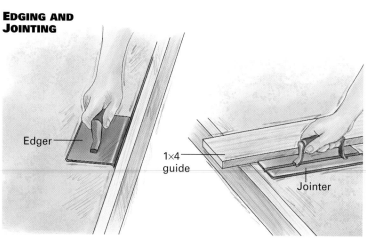

Edger

1×4 guide

Jointer

## FINISHING THE CONCRETE

Concrete finishing needs to start right after each section has been screeded.

**FLOAT THE SURFACE:** Floating levels the concrete and forces the aggregate below the surface. Most paths are narrow enough to reach from one or both sides with a wooden darby. Move the darby in overlapping arcs, keeping the leading edge slightly raised as you smooth the surface. Use light pressure and stop when water appears on the surface.

Overworking the float will bring too much water to the surface, weakening the slab.
**EDGING:** Edging rounds off the sharp corners of the slab at the forms. Rounded corners improve drainage, look better, and resist chipping. Slide a pointed trowel between the slab and the forms and work the trowel along the forms, breaking the bond. Run an edging tool back and forth between the forms, keeping the leading edge up.
**MAKE CONTROL JOINTS:** Control joints are grooves cut in the surface of the concrete. They create a place for stresses in the slab to make cracks below the surface, not on top. Form control joints at intervals equal to 1½ times the width of the walk (every 4½ feet for a 3-foot walk).

Lay a straight 1×4 perpendicular to the path; use it as a guide to scribe a line in the concrete with a pointed trowel. Set the jointing tool in the line and place the 1×4 against the edge of the tool so you guide the jointer along the line. Run the jointer back and forth, keeping the leading edge raised.

## APPLYING FINAL FINISHES

Final finishes add interest to your slab, but you have to work quickly—before the

## APPLYING A BROOM FINISH

Use a coarse, stiff-bristled broom, pulling it toward you. Work in sections without overlapping.

## SURFACE FINISHES

### TRAVERTINE

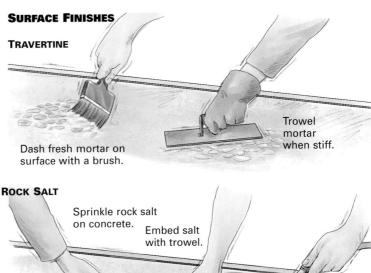

Dash fresh mortar on surface with a brush.

Trowel mortar when stiff.

### ROCK SALT

Sprinkle rock salt on concrete.

Embed salt with trowel.

Hose slab when cured to dissolve salt, leaving rough surface.

concrete sets up. Have one of your crews begin finishing a section while other sections are still being poured and screeded.

You'll know the slab is ready when the water sheen disappears, but if there is still water on the surface when the concrete begins to set, sweep the water off and begin the finishing. The illustrations above show just a few of the many finishes that will improve the look of your walk.

### CURING THE CONCRETE

Concrete should cure for five to seven days before you use it. The trick to curing is to keep the slab from drying out too quickly. Cover the slab with plastic or burlap.

## STEPS FOR EMBEDDING

1. Spread aggregate.

2. Embed stones and settle with wood float.

3. Sweep off excess concrete.

4. Wash excess concrete with fine spray.

Support weight on plywood when embedding internal patterns.

Make an aggregate finish when the concrete is still wet and workable. Work in sections right after the water sheen disappears, embedding stones so that only their upper surfaces show above the surface. Brush the surface when the concrete begins to set.

## CASTING YOUR OWN PAVERS

1. Pour concrete into mold (cut from large ice cream or other container), level it, and let it set until firm.

2. Scribe outline of stencil with screwdriver or pointed dowel. Remove stencil and scribe additional lines. Let concrete cure.

3. Remove form and set paver in path.

# GLOSSARY

**3-4-5 METHOD:** A technique for squaring corners. Done by establishing lines with mason's lines or by marking a surface, then measuring 3 feet from the corner on one line and 4 feet on the other. When the diagonal distance between the marks is 5 feet, the corner is square.

**ACTUAL DIMENSION:** The measured dimension of any material. See *Nominal dimension*.

**AGGREGATE:** Gravel or crushed rock. Often refers to the binding ingredients mixed with portland cement for concrete.

**AWL:** A sharp-pointed tool used for starting holes for wood or metal screws. Also used for scribing lines in materials.

**BACKFILL:** Soil, sand, or other material used to fill an excavation.

**BASE:** A prepared layer of gravel (and sometimes sand) to support paving material.

**BATTER BOARD:** A homemade frame of 2×4s used to lay out landscape sites.

**BOND:** The pattern formed by modular materials, such as brick, when they are laid.

**BRICK GRADE:** The rating that reflects the durability of brick, such as severe weather (SW), moderate weather (MW).

**BRICK SET:** A wide-blade, cold chisel used for cutting brick and concrete blocks.

**BUILDING CODES:** Local ordinances governing building techniques and material quality.

**BUTT JOINT:** A joint formed by two pieces of material fastened end to end, end to face, or end to edge.

**CARPENTER'S LEVEL:** A 4-foot or longer tool used to gauge when a surface is level.

**CEMENT:** A powdered mixture of lime, gypsum, and other materials used as a binding agent in concrete.

**CHAMFER:** A beveled edge.

**COMMON BRICK:** Brick manufactured for general-purpose construction. Can be used as pavement for paths in mild climates.

**CONCRETE:** A building material composed of portland cement, sand, aggregate, and water.

**CONTROL JOINT:** A groove formed in the surface of a concrete slab to prevent uncontrolled cracking.

**COURSE:** A row of paving units, such as brick or stone.

**CRUSHED STONE:** Quarried rock that has been mechanically crushed, then graded so that most of the stones are similar in size but varied in shape and color.

**CUBE OR BAND:** A quantity of paving material banded together on a pallet.

**CUT STONE:** Any of several kinds of natural rock quarried and cut into regular shapes with straight edges.

**DARBY:** A long, flat-bladed float used to smooth freshly poured concrete.

**DIMENSION LUMBER:** Lumber at least 2 inches thick and 2 inches wide.

**DOBIES:** Supports for reinforcing mesh in concrete forms.

**DRAINAGE TRENCH:** A shallow excavation used to divert water. See *Swale*.

**DRY WELL:** A hole in the soil filled with gravel, into which a drainpipe empties water.

**EDGER:** A tool used to round and smooth the edges of freshly poured concrete.

**EDGING:** A border used to contain and define the edges of a paving surface. Commonly brick, stone, lumber, plastic or steel.

**EXPOSED AGGREGATE:** A method of finishing concrete that exposes stones on top of the slab.

**FINISHING:** Any of several processes involved in smoothing concrete and giving it its final appearance.

**FLAGSTONE:** Any of several types of rock, quarried or cut from its natural surroundings and generally characterized by irregular shapes and sizes.

**FLOAT:** A rectangular wood or metal tool used for smoothing freshly poured concrete.

**FLUSH:** On the same plane as, or level with, the surrounding surface.

**FOOTING:** A small foundation, usually made of concrete, used to support a post.